New England Style

New England Style

Anna Kasabian

Foreword by Tommy Hilfiger

First published in the United States of America in 2003
by Rizzoli International Publications, Inc.
300 Park Avenue South, New York, NY 10010
www.rizzoliusa.com

©2003 by Anna Kasabian
Foreword by Tommy Hilfiger
Design by Claudia Brandenburg

2003 2004 2005 2006 2007/ 10 9 8 7 6 5 4 3 2 1

Distributed to the U.S. trade by St. Martin's Press, New York
Printed in England
ISBN: 0-8478-2583-3
Library of Congress Catalog Control Number: 2003111281

Spring p 14

Summer p 58

Fall p 114

Winter p 176

Thank you first and foremost to Tommy Hilfiger, who inspired this book and whose vision guided its creation.

Many, many thanks to three New England photographers who took the lead here—Kindra Clineff, Eric Roth, and Brian Vanden Brink. Your work captures the essence of the New England life on these pages. Many thanks as well to Sabrina Murphy, Todd Caverly, and Jody Clineff, who spent countless hours pulling together the best of the best! All of you, as well as all of the supporting photographers—Sara Gray, William Waldron, Jack McConnell, Walter Bibikow, John Gruen, Robert Holmes, Paul Rocheleau, and many others!—were the creative partners who made this happen.

Thank you to Holly Rothman for always being the calm and understanding voice who saw this through to the end. You have been wonderful to work with.

Bravo to art director Claudia Brandenburg for making this a joy to page through.

Finally, special thanks to Marilyn Williams for all her research work, project coordination, and for being a stellar organizer!

—Anna Kasabian

For David
who continues to explore,
photograph, and
taste New England with me.

Foreword
by Tommy Hilfiger

New England inspires me every day. No other part of America has played such an important role in our culture—from architecture to sea legend, sports, literature, food, and, of course, the quintessentially American preppy style that inspires fashion design around the world. Consider New England through nature's four seasons and it becomes an even richer experience. Each changing season summons new traditions and experiences that remain vivid and powerful to me even when I'm not there: Northeast Harbor's fine old shingled summer cottages, freshly baked apple pies, fishing in the Housatonic, a game of touch football on my front lawn on Nantucket Island, a clambake with friends in 'Sconset, antiquing in Litchfield, my company's first photo shoot at Moosehead Lake, or a rainy weekend spent fireside with a good book.

Even before I first set foot on Cape Cod back in the seventies, New England meant something more to me. I correctly imagined its bright blue skies, pristine beaches, the smell of pine on mossy islands, the distant sputter of a lobsterman's boat. Over the years I've had remarkable experiences there—New England offers architectural purity, a fine work ethic, long maritime and industrial histories, and a culture that produced Robert Frost, Katherine Hepburn, and the stylish and fascinating Kennedy legacy. The lifestyle there is inspired by all these contributions to New England's personality. New England is special.

Though I grew up in upstate New York, I now live primarily in Connecticut near New York City. My work keeps me away from my summer house in Nantucket more than I'd like. I think of Nantucket all of the time and my mind's eye fills with impressions of its picturesque land and seascapes. I'm transported to a slower pace where I can enjoy the better things in life: spending more time with my family and friends and appreciating Mother Nature's unique work in this corner of the world. From spring to summer, fall to winter, these are the things that make New England my home and my greatest inspiration.

If you've been to New England, I hope Anna Kasabian's beautiful book inspires another adventure. If you haven't, I hope now you'll soon make the trip. But in case you don't, please use this book as your own guide to import a little New England style into your daily life. Whether your journey is real or virtual, I know you'll enjoy the ride.

—Tommy Hilfiger

Spring

That first morning we step out the front door, the smell of warmed soil reaching into our nostrils, the yellow-green hue of new bulb shoots rising from the soil like little rockets, we are reassured that spring is not far. And regardless of what kind of a winter we have had, we turn to a blank page in our scrapbook, ready for the new views and the new memories that we'll capture on film.

No more is the frost glazing the tops of the grass blades. We move to the potting shed or barn and ready the tools that will churn up what the winter snow has packed into little cakes of fall leaves to unveil a new season's growing soil. We plan and plot our gardens, start our seeds, and prune back what the year's storms have snapped.

Inside we pile the warm wool throws and ski sweaters and send them to the attic to wait out the good weather to come. Down come the cotton throws, the summer wardrobe, and the cheery prints that will adorn our tabletops and lighten our window frames.

If you drive the back roads of New England now, the sky sits pale and serene against the new growth pastures. New calves waddle unsteady behind their mothers, as do new additions to the sheep flock. Farm ponds ripple under the little duck trains that swirl and dip, mother duck in the lead. Riders saddle up their horses and get ready for a good run through the soft spring soil. The rivers from Maine to New Hampshire, swollen from the melt, will soon be full of fisher-men and explored by canoes and kayaks. It is a beautiful time to be in New England.

Vineyard Escape

With no chance of a frost in sight and easier seas to navigate, the owners and caretakers of summer places on Martha's Vineyard rejoice. They come by plane or ferry to officially open their homes. They may tag on an extra day, maybe two, to clean the garden and get their patio furniture out, prepping for their first outdoor breakfast.

Shutters that may have locked out the winter winds are peeled back, as are the snowy-white sheets that formed protective glaciers of cotton on the furniture indoors. Potting sheds, sealed off from frigid air and ice storms, are opened. With that first ray of sun peeping in, the dank, cool, coffinned air is released and we get a whiff of last summer's spicy soil. Stacks of terra-cotta pots, the copper birdbath, and Grandma's old trellis are carried one by one to their familiar spaces—on the patio, porch, or under the pergola.

Windows are opened, letting the sea-seasoned air flow through the house, a little tornado of freshness to scrub the corners of our rooms. Bed linens and our favorite old blankets cocoon the beds; beach blankets, beach chairs, and our outdoor games come together again.

It's a wonderful time to be here to take in the quiet. There is little traffic on the road—or in the water—and the restaurants, beaches, and villages are calm for the moment.

This is a good time too to see the sites sans crowds. Take a sailboat out for the day and cruise to the harbors and by the beaches. You will have the rare opportunity to see the details of the towns, the architecture, and the contours of the beach. Clock the day by how many lighthouses you pass, and plan to picnic on a barren beach. The cry of the gull and the ocean's foaming will be the only sounds you'll hear.

Sailing and yachting are natural pastimes here. The Vineyard Haven Yacht Club opened in 1928 and continues today to offer families sailing lessons and competitive events throughout the summer. Their races have whizzed past island markers like the West Chop Lighthouse for a few generations.

With rough seas surrounding the Vineyard, lighthouses have been safety beacons for ships coming into port as far back as the 1600s. There are five, all on the north shore, that look out over Vineyard Sound at Gay Head and West Chop, and over Nantucket Sound at East Chop (in Oak Bluffs), Edgartown Harbor, and Cape Pogue (Chappaquiddick). The West Chop Lighthouse in Vineyard Haven has been a port of protection since 1645. The red-brick Gay Head lighthouse is a great place to watch the sunset. East Chop Lighthouse in Oak Bluffs is on the site of one of the first telegraph signals set up in 1828. Until it was painted white, it was called the Chocolate Lighthouse. The original Edgartown Lighthouse was built in 1828 on a man-made island. The most remote, Cape Pogue, was replaced four times, always destroyed by wild seas. Go by moped or bike; take a picnic, camera, easel, or sketchbook. Lighthouses are the essence of island spirit.

Spring is also a good time to bike the island. Without the summer crowds, it's a pleasure to have the roads and paths to yourself. Take advantage of the peace and quiet and pack your camera, sketch pad, or travel easel and move around until you find what turns your creative spirit on.

There's nothing quite like waking up in a beachside inn and trekking down to the sand dunes. Whether you're on the dunes at National Seashore in Wellfleet, Race Point in Provincetown, or Nantucket's Dionis beach, just three miles from the center of town, you are at the center of summer life on the Cape and the islands. Footpaths in Wellfleet lead to the dunes, where at high tide you'll be ankle-deep in water and your toes will feel the fizz of crabs bobbing and popping up from beneath the sand. And at low tide, if you're at the top of a dune, you can see thin ribbons of beach wind and curl a quarter mile away. Sometimes when you sit there, you and your pup are the only breathing creatures. The sand is like powder underfoot and the sea grass sways in front of you, waving summer on. Don't miss the dunes.

Go to a place that's quiet, and sit for awhile. Watch spring's new light, smells and sounds. It's a gentle massage on your wintered senses.

The burgeoning of spring on Martha's Vineyard, or any other New England island from Monhegan to Nantucket, is a dramatic and emotional time. All of us are craving warm sun, the familiar rhythmic sound of our porch swings and rockers, and the flutter of new birds at our feeders. One place, though, that declares to us that the cold is long gone is Oak Bluffs. Stroll the neighborhoods full of gingerbread cottages; the bright blues, hot pinks, and apple green laced in crisp white carvings, the porches lined in wicker, and the spring flowers opening make the point so perfectly.

Nothing welcomes spring with more local color than the annual Daffodil Festival on Nantucket island. Every spring these striking yellow-petaled rockets shoot from the ground, and like sequins sewn onto green silk, they detail the landscape for miles. The tradition of the festival goes back to 1974 and Jean MacAusland, who gave a million or so daffodil bulbs to the island and invited volunteers to plant them. And unlike the tulip, these bright-yellow beauties would not turn into dinner for the local deer and rabbits. Townspeople took to the idea and planted them everywhere. If you visit during the festival, you can see them on display in Main Street shop windows, at a flower show, and at many of the island's inns.

A
Lobsterman's Pier

Fishing piers from Bearskin Neck in Rockport, Massachusetts, to Ogunquit, Maine, share those common postcard views of grayed and weathered shacks, dried over the years from the hot sun and salty air, adorned with gumdrop-colored buoys.

If you get out there early enough in the day, before the tourists or beachgoers pack up their pleasure boats, you'll likely pass fishermen and lobstermen, donning their bright yellow garb, readying for a day at sea. The only sounds are the cry of the gull and the rhythmic clanging of the ship's bell.

They can only hope the day will bring decent weather—no fog patches—and traps so full that they make the men's arms ache by the time they pull up number five. Listen for the deep gurgle of their boat engines starting up—the sputter, the cough—and when the smell of gasoline is thick in the air, they'll be off, a parade out to sea. The gulls will undoubtedly follow, circling and crying their high-pitched wail, knowing full well an easy breakfast is just minutes away.

When the lobstermen and fishermen return, the clam and lobster shacks—like Mabel's Lobster Claw in Kennebunkport—and local restaurants quickly pass those gifts from the sea into their kitchens. Piles of lobsters will soon become sweet white meat landing on a paper plate; corn-on-the-cob, fries, and slaw complete that familiar fair-weather menu.

As you drive the coast of New England you will find hundreds of roadside stands with this fresh bounty being boiled, stuffed, and baked up. You can tell by the lines snaking out the door who has the best fryers in the kitchen, who has the tastiest batters.

Some, like Ipswich's Clam Box, are even shaped like a clam box so you can't miss them! Most, like the Clam Box, Woodman's, the Village Restaurant, and Farnhams, all of Essex, Massachusetts, are so successful they have been around for decades, serving generations of the same family. Each and every one has its faithful followers, customers who will drive an hour or more for their favorite stand's style and specialties.

Woodman's has been serving seafood since the early 1900s. And like most lobster shacks, it lets you pick your own lobster from the pool outside and enjoy a cool beer while you wait. It's not ritzy—none of the best places really are. These stands are the only place to go after a day at the beach, when shorts are pulled up over swimsuits and the smell of sunscreen is thick in the car.

At Woodman's, as at many others, there is a screened-in porch free of flies and picnic tables out back for when the biting greenhead flies are long gone. The mix of sea air and smells from the fryers define the whole experience. On the perfect spring or summer day, you'll likely be in a long lobster line that extends down Main Street. You'll catch a glimpse of the boats heading downriver and the steady stream of cars in search of the beach or the next stand, which may have a shorter line.

They're used to serving lots of plates at Woodman's. In 1988 they served up a clambake to the players of the U.S. Open Golf Tournament—right on the sixth hole—held at The Country Club in Brookline, Massachusetts, right across the street. And in 1999 they did it again at Boston's Fenway Park, feeding 3,500 guests at the All-Star Game.

The roots of the place go back to 1912 when Chubby Woodman, after losing his job, started digging clams to earn money. On his first day he got himself three bushels that sold for a dollar each. And the rest, as they say, is history.

His first experiments with frying clams came two years later, just before the Fourth of July. After deep-frying some potatoes, he threw a whole clam into the oil and it exploded. Then he shucked it, dipped it in a batter, and tried again. That was in 1916, and the family has been frying clams and boiling lobster ever since.

Beachside clambakes started at Woodman's when the wealthy families in the area called on Chubby to serve their guests on the beach. He discovered that digging a pit for a wood fire in the sand and covering it with an old bed frame was the perfect setup for boiling up chowder, lobster, clams, corn, and hot dogs.

This is the kind of scene that makes a fishing pier art. We may paint it, photograph it, or use it as the scene in a novel. It's a defining moment in time.

Lobster is as common in New England as a side of ketchup. At Farnham's, established circa 1942, a few minutes north of the village of Essex, Massachusetts, in the direction of Gloucester, they make a mean lobster roll. The little white restaurant sits at the edge of the water with Ipswich visible in the distance and has a postcard view of an old summer house that looks like an Andrew Wyeth painting. Step inside, and the knotty pine walls, snug little booths, and sea breezes coming through make you feel very, very far from the buzz of daily life. Owners Terry and Joe Cellucci hold the Farnham family's secret recipes. Here, they share their lobster roll recipe.

FARNHAM'S LOBSTER ROLL
*Lobster meat from the Manchester Lobster Company
*Cut into chunks.
*Toss with Cain's Real Mayonnaise only when you're ready to stuff it into a roll. Make this fresh!
*Shred fresh iceberg lettuce and put on the bottom of a slightly grilled hot dog roll. Top it all with the lobster mix. Voila! A little concerto for your taste buds.

Did you know that a traditional New England clambake includes lobsters, potatoes, corn-on-the-cob, clams, and chowder? You could actually make up your own clambake tour of the region, starting at the Connecticut shore's take-out stands and moving all the way north to Castine, Maine, where you can sit on the pier and have some of New England's finest lobster.

Get ready to put on a plastic bib with a big red lobster on it and double up your paper plate. This is going to be one juicy meal. Perhaps the screams from diners soaked to the core after their plates collapse on their laps will be the best reminder! And if you don't know how to eat a lobster, get the clam shack owner to break it up for you. Some places even print up instructions. You will be supplied with a nutcracker, pick, and whatever else the place thinks you'll need to get into this delicious crustacean. Oh, and don't eat anything you aren't sure about. Ask about the green and red stuff; for some it's a delicacy, for others a turnoff.

The best accompaniments to the shellfish feast are a cold beer and a dessert of watermelon—unless, of course, you've chosen a place that has homemade ice cream or pies made with locally grown berries.

Now, for those who want to create an authentic beachside clambake, here are instructions from the experts at Woodman's of Essex, Massachusetts.

First, make your chowder at home and bring a big pot, which will first be the vessel for heating the chowder, and later the pan to boil lobsters in. Be sure to bring plenty of fresh water from home for boiling the lobsters as well as butter to dip them in.

As soon as you arrive at the beach, dig a big hole in the sand. Build a wood fire in it, and then top it with a bunch of boulders and fieldstones that will get red-hot.

Next, lay down a layer of wet seaweed. Add a layer of potatoes, since they take the longest to cook, and cover them with seaweed. Then create additional layers of potatoes, clams, and corn. Cover the whole thing with canvas and relax while everything steams. Some people steam the lobster too, but Woodman's recommends that you boil it. Add a good amount of salt to the water, and boil. Soft-shell lobsters should be cooked for eight to ten minutes, hard-shell for twelve to fifteen minutes. Shells are hard in winter, soft in spring, and get harder as summer comes.

Serve the lobsters with plenty of melted butter and clam broth on the side. The idea is to swish the clams around in broth to clean off any clinging sand.

As the light of day fades and the party quiets down, watch the stars come out and the moon pass by.

A CONVERTED

Boathouse

In our quest to preserve and honor the past, we often end up living, vacationing, or even shopping in places that originally had other purposes, other lives. It is not uncommon to find carriage houses or stables, in the city or the country, that have been transformed into stores or homes. And it is just as easy to discover churches, boathouses, lighthouses, and old gristmills functioning as homes or inns. For New England's architects, restoration builders, or carpenters this offers thousands of interesting projects—projects that will be passed on to future generations who will hold these precious places close to their hearts.

Groups like the Society for the Preservation of New England Antiquities (SPNEA) and the Trustees of Reservations protect the most prestigious, historically significant property collections and give us access to the gardens, mansions, and farmhouses that have captured the essence of the region's history and its families. Visiting these homes—from the Crane Estate in Ipswich, Massachusetts, to Roseland Cottage in Woodstock, Connecticut—inspires us in our own home design and decor.

We live in and visit these places to change our perspective, perhaps to leave our high-tech, nontextural lives behind for at least part of our days. If we choose to live in a house from the 1600s, we may design the interiors to keep all the remnants of modern life out of sight. Architects help to hide the wires and systems that cue us that it's the twenty-first century. Designers help us track down the details, from period sconces and old marble sinks to faithful period reproductions. At the North Bennet Street School in Boston's North End, the skills of fine woodworking and preservation carpentry are taught, and graduates produce handmade

Here is the perfect escape—
an old boathouse given new life
as a getaway. The setting
and the space give us the texture,
scenery, and salt air we crave
all the workweek long.

When we carefully transform these places—open them to the light of day—and reveal the views, we are sustained by the simple pleasure of staring off to sea and letting the sea breezes in.

furnishings that, like the pieces they seek to duplicate, will themselves become precious heirlooms someday. In its hundred-plus-year history, the school has remained committed to training people in time-honored methods and skills that produce the finely crafted products New Englanders love.

Let us not forget that all of this is rooted in an appreciation for the past, for the craftspeople who carved the wood, cut the glass, and tapped each and every nail into place to build our rooms and create the views that take us out of our element.

The Keeper's House Inn on Isle Au Haut Bay, Maine, is protected by the National Registrar of Historic Places. Guests arrive by mail boat, and then innkeepers Jeff and Judi Burke give them a unique taste of New England. By day you enjoy the scenery, and the deer, osprey, seal, and porpoise who will undoubtedly visit. There is no electricity, no telephone, and nothing much to do. Candles, kerosene, and gas lamps light the

way when darkness falls. To lie in bed at night, listen to the ocean, and think that the lighthouse keeper once walked these halls is truly something you will never forget.

Or take this nineteenth-century boathouse on Little Diamond Island, Maine. In the 1800s it served as a Coast Guard coaling station, and later it housed the island convenience store and gas pumps. Just a fifteen-minute boat ride from Portland, where trendy new restaurants and shops are popping up regularly, this retreat is a place that gives its owner breathing space and a good dose of nature as well. Today the space has a new life as a special hideaway, and New England architect Rob Whitten helped bring it back to life. It's not hard to imagine that this was once filled with fishing and lobster gear and winches. That was the idea, really—to keep the feel of an old Maine boathouse, introduce a few modern comforts, and maybe house the owner's boat-building project someday.

DREAMING ON

The Porch

It seems like spring never comes fast enough in New England. While we natives thrive on all four seasons, nothing is quite as dramatic for us as the arrival of spring. From that first morning when we can set off to the porch or patio, pajama-clad, coffee in one hand, and swing open the door, we declare winter's passing.

Soon we'll sweep the remnants of fall leaves out the door and set down the rocking chairs, plant stands, and sun-faded floral pillows on our favorite wicker chair. We will move through our happy rituals that ready this place for family and friends: displaying last summer's shell collection, filling an old hand-blown vase from the cupboard and setting it, just like last season, on the railing that wraps the porch. The brass dinner bell will get shined up, and new candles will go onto the tables in anticipation of a spring feast porch-side, as dusk falls. Perhaps we will paint the steps and floor again—high gloss white to reflect the spring sky—and trim back the forsythia to open our view. The window boxes will be hung and filled to the brim with hardy, colorful mixes. And we will wait patiently for our old rose bushes to bloom, for the clematis to trail down the wall.

Our palettes are dramatic as we push winter's gray landscape far, far away. With long, snowy winters and chilly springs that sometimes last through mid-June, these outdoor rooms are cherished spaces that ease us into a new time and a new season. As we sit, curled up with a paperback or sketchbook, looking out to the harbor front, the pasture, or Main Street, the day goes by.

We use the structures, from pergolas to potting sheds, archways and gates, pavers and paths, as the base for our landscape art and plant them as well. Local granite or marble may make up the weaving, twisted paths that lead to patio seating areas, kitchen cutting or herb gardens, or a cluster of fruit trees.

You can find some of the most beautiful private and public porches woven into the main streets and in the village centers of coastal communities, such as Essex, Connecticut, and Edgartown on Martha's Vineyard. They're appended to and often wrap around the private homes, restaurants, and inns, and the spectacular museum homes like the Mark Twain homestead in Hartford. The styles are mixed—Greek Revival, English-style cottages, rural gothic, shingle-style, and tower cottages.

Others are integral to the experience of our old resorts and inns, many of which offer up, from the porch or veranda, the most beautiful garden, ocean, and mountain views in New England. Families who make the annual trek to their favorite inns or resorts over the years probably have their favorite corners where the view never changes.

The covered porch at the Red Lion Inn in Stockbridge, Massachusetts, is lined with rockers and chairs as soon as the weather complies. From the porch at the Balsams in Dixville Notch, New Hampshire, you have endless open views of the countryside. From the porch or patio at the Basin Harbor Club in Vergennes, Vermont, there are serene views of Lake Champlain, and from the Colony's grand covered porch in Kennebunkport, Maine, you can look out on the open ocean. But perhaps the prettiest gardens and pathways, though, are at Edgartown's Charlotte Inn. Every turn you take in their garden paths is picture-perfect. These porches and patios, some over a hundred years old, have seen several generations of a family rocking in their chairs and running down their stone paths.

Our porches welcome the season's arrival. And when we sit there that first warm day, the view contained in a carved wood frame, we snap shots as we scan the harbor.

THE

Gardener's Shed

When spring comes, the New England gardener puts the books on bulbs aside and heads for the potting shed. These great little hideaways come in many forms, sizes, and shapes.

It could be an empty end stall in the barn transformed into our seed and garden tool sanctuary. Or a falling-down chicken coop that, with the help of a local carpenter, has been brought to a new place, with a new purpose.

Sometimes we append the potting shed to the house, connecting it by way of the mudroom. It could be a new building we construct with reclaimed barn wood, windows from a church, and shelves that once lined a hundred-year-old library's walls. There might be one stained glass window that buttons a solid wall. That way when the sun shines on our work table, ribbons of color come across our pots and tools, reminding us of the blooms to come.

Look around as you tour the country lanes this time of year. The potting shed or some form of garden room will be visible. Chances are, the door will be wide open. Some are merged rooms within the greenhouse or conservatory, whether they are authentic, period reproductions, or a little of both. There are people around who collect the bones of collapsed or abandoned greenhouses and rebuild them.

Some of these places are stand-alone designs with their own stone paths to the front door, their own fences bordering their space. Or they may be a woodshed that went with the house, and is now painted and shuttered to match.

They are not just country places, either. In Boston those who live at the rooftop level have gardens and garden sheds that overlook the city. On Beacon Hill there may be a hundred or more hidden gardens and sheds. They're tucked behind the high brick walls and big wooden doors that wrap the Hill's gaslit streets and cobblestone paths.

Spring is a good time to look for flea market finds for the garden. It's amazing what we recycle—mismatched dishes and cups to hold seeds, milking pails that can hold soils, grass seed, and garden tools. We are known to shop at our own neighbor's garage sales. At spring-cleaning time we New Englanders empty out our attics and cellars and bring the contents to the front lawn. Paint an orphan desk drawer and you have yourself a place to stash seeds.

Roadside stands and nurseries are all over the region, and many areas these days have farmer's markets. These gather the farmers and their goods in one place, making it easy for locals and visitors to buy right from the source. In-season produce, flowers, plants, and locally grown meats come by truck or van to the town center for a few hours on weekends.

The ingredients of the gardener's shed do not vary much; it is the details and the owner's style that distinguish one from another—the choice of containers, the shelving, the color inside and out. These are as individual as the gardeners and their plantings. Certainly too, in true New England form, we may still have the trowel, shovel, or seed box of our grandmother or great uncle. So we carry these through life and pack and unpack them season after season. We may frame Grandma's seed list, the one she always kept in her shed, or wear her garden gloves for good luck. If we are lucky enough, we have a plant pot or two, or maybe even a garden gate from family gardens.

Step into one of these places in the spring and you will likely find the gardener's shoes—maybe those brightly colored rubber clogs—and not too far away, planting diagrams tucked into a cubby made from an old mail sorter from the post office. Barn-board shelves, or perhaps a wall of mailboxes, store everything from fertilizers, glass spray bottles, bug spray, and citronella candles to tools and seeds. There's probably a big bin full of fresh soil around, ready for starting the seeds and replenishing the garden beds. Somewhere, perhaps on an old kitchen table being used as a work surface, there is a stack of vases, pots, window boxes, watering cans, and popsicle sticks that will be transformed into little signs that label the rows in the gardens.

If you need inspiration on what to plant or how to design your garden shed, there are many options. Visiting gardens and nurseries in New England is a wonderful way to study what does well in water, seaside, or in wildflower gardens. Visit the White Flower Farm if you can in Litchfield, Connecticut, where you can walk the property and study the marked beds of flowers and groundcovers. And for your own garden-shed supplies, there is a store there as well. Make sure you take a catalog or visit them online if you want to take time with your selections. At the Vermont Wildflower Farm between Burlington and Middlebury, there are more than 250 varieties of wildflowers to see on six acres of land. Everything is labeled here, too, so as you walk the grounds you can learn as you look, and keep a list of your favorites. Then you can just head for the seed store.

Also some of the region's most beautiful public gardens, as well as inn and resort gardens, will inspire you. In Massachusetts alone, the historic homes have beautiful gardens in a variety of styles: the Codman Estate in Lincoln; Stevens-Coolidge Place in North Andover; Mission House, Stockbridge; and Long Hill in Beverly. The Inn at Castle Hill, Ipswich, with views to the ocean, is planted nicely, and touring the property of the neighboring Crane Estate will give you plenty of gardens and landscaping to study. There is also the Guest House at Field Farm in Williamstown with sculpture gardens.

Take an afternoon to stroll in Boston's Public Garden and visit the nearby Arnold Arboretum to give yourself an education on all of the unusual trees that thrive here. Of course, if you can see the city's magnolia trees in blossom—a straight pink line for seven city blocks—you just might plant a few in your yard.

Choose a state or two that you would like to visit and plan to stop in their nurseries, as well as visit their gardens and estates. Each state has an abundance of both, each with its own character and landscapes—and whatever you see will get you to a better supplied garden shed and an interesting garden.

If you are lucky, there will be a hatch, just as you throw your line into the Housatonic River out in western Massachusetts, and before you get a bead of sweat on your brow, you will feel the tug of the trout. There are more than 100,000 acres of outdoor spaces to hunt, hike, canoe, and camp in New England. For the fly fisherman, trout, perch, and bass are there for the taking, and they say for some of the best fly fishing you should head to the river's edge in northwestern Connecticut. If you're really passionate about this peaceful sport, visit the American Museum of Fly Fishing in Manchester, Vermont. You'll see the gear that Ernest Hemingway, Herbert Hoover, Babe Ruth, and even Glenn Miller used, not to mention the Prince of Wales' vest.

Summer

Summering in New England is the stuff of paperback novels. The characters and settings are all here, and once we choose our destination, our cottage—one room or ten, by the sea or lake—we ready ourselves to become part of the place. In Provincetown, Massachusetts, you can rent a ramshackle weathered place where high tide comes up to the porch chairs; at low tide, you and your dog can walk the pressed sand for half an hour before you touch water. On Sebago Lake, Maine, you can wake in a hundred-year-old cottage, and take your breakfast at the lodge by the fire every day for a dozen days. Or perhaps you will be on the shore of Lake Champlain, Vermont, on the manicured lawn of the Basin Harbor Club, perched in a gumdrop-colored chair watching the day begin. We sink into wonderful rituals in summer. We take the same route to that favorite place with the same picnic, packed and ready for the road break we always take.

Some people take the same cottage or room for years and years. It's that familiarity, the halls and turns in the place we've memorized, and the summer menus that never change. It is all this that gets us to unwind as fast as little tops. If we head for the family's summer house, we each have our rooms, old friends that they are. We wouldn't think of changing that view, our view. Besides, we know just how to set the book under the window, so the window doesn't slam down during a summer storm. It's been that way for ten summers or more. Summer in New England is about going back to a place we love and doing the things that keep us in a special rhythm.

THE

Sea Captain's House

New England's coastal and island towns hold beautiful collections of home styles, preserved and maintained with the utmost care. Some are set back on impressive hills, overlooking the town and village harbors; others are tucked off little footpaths near the sea, and still others, like those in Newburyport, sit one after the other, on smaller plots of land on the main street.

But it is the sea captain's homes that are often some of the most impressive specimens you will find, from Maine to the island of Nantucket. The wealthier sea captains spared nothing to make these majestic places, hiring the best craftspeople they could find to fill their homes with grand, winding staircases, intricately carved wall panels and mantels, and hand-painted tiles. Period wallpapers or hand-painted walls brought color to the halls and public rooms. When there was land available, they created colorful gardens that presented them with views they could enjoy year-round. Fabrics, furnishings, and collectibles from their travels around the world found their way into living rooms, parlors, libraries, and bedrooms.

Sea captains called upon architects to build in a variety of styles—whatever was their fancy—from Greek and Georgian Revivals to Second Empire. In Salem, Massachusetts, which in 1790 was, per capita, the richest city in the country, there are examples of all of these. Earlier homes like the 1668 home of Captain John Turner, now the House of Seven Gables, is a stunning specimen, as is the city's oldest brick house, the 1762 home Captain John Derby built for his son.

Stroll Nantucket Town to see some examples of seaside architecture and many a sea captain's nest.

The sailing theme in the decor here recalls the roots of this special place.

The man who reaped the benefits of Turner's and Derby's success and desires was Salem architect and woodcarver Samuel McIntire. Just stroll around the green, opposite the Hawthorne Inn, and you will see many of these creations, punctuation points for a special time in history.

You will find the same as you drive north on Route 1-A in Newburyport and see huge, white homes with the familiar widow's walk perched on top. Step inside and you will find beautiful hardwood floors, massive fireplaces, perhaps ten to a house, century-old floor tiles in the hall, secret stairways, and doors with knockers that are heavy in your hand. Head south to Old Town Marblehead and you will find more. The streets here are narrow, climbing and winding around the water's edge. The mix of architecture is a history lover's paradise.

The architectural culture clash of simple Quaker style and the wealthy nineteenth-century homes of sea captains and merchants has proved a recipe for postcard-perfect charm for this Nantucket town. Main Street and the side streets are woven with these

studies in the island's social history. Clapboard-and-shingle Quaker homes with white picket fences, black shutters, center chimneys, and neat-as-a-pin garden spaces sit beside the grand and ornate sea captains' homes, wrapped in milky-white clapboard and black shutters—true gifts from the surrounding sea.

Truth is, the simple, beautiful craftsmanship of the Quakers was lost, as was the hold their religion had on the island. The wealth that came with being a whaling metropolis opened new ways of thinking, and eventually a new canvas for the builders, artisans, and craftsmen. Ornament replaced utilitarianism.

The house pictured here, built in 1826 by Captain Seth Pinkham, is modest compared to some of Salem's and Newburyport's sea captains' homes. Its caretakers today have chosen to keep the design elements simple, like the structure, with consistent themes of the sea and sailing.

With the abundance of antique stores trailing up the coast, it is easy to find the design details that complement a theme or a time and place that we want to hold in our rooms.

With the sea so prominent in our history and a part of life today, it is no wonder that the bright colors of the flags, blue sky, and woody details of the yachts and ships that carry us come into our living spaces. We hunt down the nautical prints, the ship's manifest, the captain's diary, and we frame or display them. There are collectors and shops all over New England that help us find the ship's bell, the captain's clock, and the old brass instruments that will sit on our nightstands or hang in our halls, special markers of the time spent at sea.

THE IDEAL

Summer Retreat

Our summer places allow us to create environments that give us breathing space for our personal style. We can create our own fantasy, one that might suggest the setting or, in our choice of decor, the period in which the cottage or house was built. We can shape a place so that it contrasts so much so with our winter homes that we feel very, very far away from our reality. It is the same reason we choose one inn over another—the farm vacation in Maine instead of the converted mansion in Vermont. One satisfies our sense of escape more than the other.

We may choose a summer place by the sea because the sound of the foghorn and waves soothe us in a special way; they call to us. Or it may be that waking lakeside to the cry of the loon appeals to us because it recalls the setting of a favorite paperback we read years ago. Just as regions click with people, so do certain houses. Maybe we choose a rambling old summer house on Vinalhaven Island, Maine, because it reminds us of our childhood summer place. Or, perhaps the porch resembles the one at our favorite inn, where we sat at dawn every day for a week.

Sometimes it's just love at first sight, which was the case at Boulderwood, built in 1900 in Stockbridge, Massachusetts, and once the summer home of the Farnham family. Today's owner, Jim Finnerty, dreamed his whole life about owning this beautiful architectural specimen. He could not get it out of his mind from the time he spent an entire summer painting it when he was a college student. The light, the views, and the place just spoke to his soul. One day, at the right time, it went up for sale. With careful decorating decisions—finding everything from paintings to accent pieces at flea markets and auctions—Finnerty has made Boulderwood feel like time has stood still. He can doze on his sleeping porch and listen to the summer breeze or sit by the stone fireplace on a winter's day and daydream. A few rooms in this special place have been opened to guests who can visit any season to create their own special memories of Boulderwood.

We want to capture that mood; we want those views we read about or once saw. And to fit in the place—the picture, if you will—we begin to collect what we want to bring there, things that will bring that feeling to life. So it will become a place that we can sink into, and when we close the front door, we can cocoon ourselves from reality for a little while.

To that end, it could be that we find some antique linens with embroidered shells in the corners. Or maybe on a drive through Wiscasset, Maine, we come across an estate sale and, there, in a pile of old prints, is one of a hotel that once served the island's summer residents. On another adventure we find a collection of sea glass that we imagine will work perfectly in our island house.

If our escape is an eighteenth-century farmhouse in Lincolnville, Maine, our design hunt changes. Our grandmother's old canning jars might be perfect for dry beans, and lining the pantry shelves with them will remind us of her. A day trip to Grafton, Vermont, may bring us to a potter's shop where farm-style pots inspire a theme for the front stoop. We take a flea market find, like a long-retired milking stool, and use it to reach high places in our library. And some winter's day when we can't resist the sleigh bells jingling, inviting us into a cozy shop, we come across a trio of pitchforks that could be the perfect art for a back-hall stairway. They come home with us, as does the spinning wheel.

Thankfully, in New England there are collectors and antique dealers who sell just about anything imaginable. So it is not difficult to turn your summer home or weekend escape into a place that embraces its setting and its history. And if you remain in hunt mode year-round, collecting themed decorative pieces, you can seed them throughout your home.

The home pictured here once belonged to a Nantucket whaling captain. Today the owners who summer here found a pleasing balance in bringing in items that subtly suggest the sea. There are glass buoys on the floor, rope and wood furniture, portraits of naval officers, and pictures of sailing vessels. Simple, clean-lined furnishings like the bedroom set and dining room table and chairs keep the place casual and don't detract from the character of the place. The old wood floors, moldings, and other architectural details stand out. Shuttered windows that take in the sea breeze frame the views.

Here is the purest form of New England's summer home style. Simple and understated, it dovetails perfectly with the landscape.

So often we take a place's point in history and embrace it inside and out. Old houses speak to us, and those with a passion for them listen very hard.

Walk into Boulderwood today and you can just imagine what the summer was like here in 1900. The views down the mountain are the same, the refurbished interior carries the spirit of the time.

If you've never dug your own clams for a summer's lunch, you are missing a part of the season's experience that can really soothe your soul. Your high-tech world will seem far away. All that's required is getting down into the sand with your rake and pail to hunt down the little holes that hide a stack of luncheon delights. For inspiration and instruction, read Christopher Reaske's books *The Compleat Clammer* or *The Compleat Crab and Lobster.* Or, hop on your bike, find some clammers, and watch them work. And don't forget to go to the town hall for a license!

THE

Rose Grower's Cottage

Nantucket Island's rose-covered cottages make it a storybook kind of place. If the weather has been accommodating, the blossoms are plentiful, full and intoxicating. They're strung across white picket fences, providing a lush pink-and-green frame to the cottages and inns here, and they have, over the years, become one of the visual calling cards of this enchanting island.

They twist in and out and over arbors. Their blankets of pink drape cottage roofs. And the views they make from near and far have been captured on miles of film and memorialized on note cards and calendars. The views they create put painters to their easels and watercolor papers. We just don't want to forget what we see here.

On a bluff overlooking the ocean, on the easternmost tip of the island, the ten rose-covered cottages of Summer House in Siasconset draw guests year after year who crave these special picturesque getaways.

With the right design ingredients, you can create a Nantucket-style garden scene wherever roses can grow. Visit a garden center to discuss your dream rose garden or meet with a landscape architect who can sketch out exactly where she would plant your bushes and climbers. There are varieties for the front of your house, along the fence, and next to the arbor that can serve as the entryway to your home or backyard garden.

Pick up a copy of Lewis and Nancy Hill's *The Flower Gardener's Bible* for some practical advice on choosing and growing roses. They point out that the large-flowered climbers and hybrid wichurana can be trained to grow along fences or up trellises and arbors. The bloom of another type of rose—the rambler rose—

You can create your own Nantucket-style garden by choosing the right rose varieties, fencing and arbors.

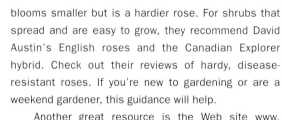

blooms smaller but is a hardier rose. For shrubs that spread and are easy to grow, they recommend David Austin's English roses and the Canadian Explorer hybrid. Check out their reviews of hardy, disease-resistant roses. If you're new to gardening or are a weekend gardener, this guidance will help.

Another great resource is the Web site www. heirloomroses.com, which reviews rose varieties and provides all the information you need on growing zones. For fresh design ideas and advice, page through *Country Living Gardener* or *Garden Design* magazines.

To complete the look, investigate options like antique brick or stone for your walkways, and visit the New England Arbors Web site (www.newenglandarbors.com), which has an abundance of picket fences, arbors, gates, and trellises in the styles you see on the island.

With a little planning, you can create beautiful Nantucket-style views for your home—inside and out. Imagine waking up in the morning and looking out your window at a cluster of pink coming up the sill. Or perhaps your roses will climb and wind over the arbor in the distance that leads to the sandy beach of your summer home.

And when winter comes and little tufts of snow frost the top of the picket fence and lacey wall arbor, you'll dream about the pink buds that will come someday soon.

If you haven't heard of Nantucket Reds, you probably haven't spent much time on the island. Philip C. Murray, the original owner of Murray's Toggery, is the man behind the color and the fabric. He started selling brick-red sailcloth men's slacks in the 1940s. They caught on fire, and Philip gave them the name that is known, they say, the world over. Murray's Toggery is more than just a place to shop, though. You come here to say hello to your neighbors, catch up on their lives, and maybe set a golf date.

Just as we return, little family flocks, to our beach houses, lakeside retreats, and resorts, we go back to our favorite playgrounds as well. When it's time for a sail around the lake island, we know the boathouse will have number 1207 next to 1206, all lined up, just like last year. We can count on our favorite resort to have the croquet games and shuffleboard equipment ready to go. And best of all, we know the views from these waterfront lawns are as beautiful as ever.

THE ISLAND

Lighthouse

If you were to fly low over the New England shoreline at night, the blinking lighthouse beacons would appear like a string of holiday lights below. These sturdy, sometimes weathered clapboard structures, outlined in the blue sky, perch high above the sea like little compass faces.

For the lighthouse keepers, these have been somewhat lonely workplaces, no matter how breathtaking the setting. Lighthouses are the stuff of legends, folklore, and many a book. Some writers track the lighthouses' beginnings and follow their history, and others choose them as the scene of a crime in a mystery novel.

As structures, they are cherished pieces of history—markers of drowned ships, saved ships, the captains, and their crews. Today numerous groups watch over them and work to restore and preserve them.

Many lighthouses now welcome guests for overnight stays: the Keeper's House in Isle Au Haut at Acadia National Park, in Maine; the Lighthouse Inn, in West Dennis, Massachusetts; Monomoy Point off Chatham, Massachusetts; Popham Beach Bed and Breakfast, Race Point, Provincetown, on Cape Cod; Rose Island in Newport Harbor, Rhode Island; and Thatcher Island in Cape Ann, Massachusetts. Depending on where you choose to stay and live a day or two of fantasy, you may get gourmet food and canopied beds, or at Rose Island, be assigned some lightkeeper's responsibilities and rough it a bit.

We can turn a room into a place the lighthouse keeper would easily recognize.

These lighthouses were workplaces and, given their location, furnished with just the basics. If there were decorative things brought in—there were female lighthouse keepers, by the way!—it is likely that they came as things found: seashells that washed up, interesting rocks, sea glass, driftwood, and whalebones, things that perhaps floated to shore from a wreck. Little anonymous treasures that could line a shelf or windowsill and add to the view.

You can re-create the mood of a lighthouse keeper's kitchen by finishing your space with bead board walls and reclaimed wood flooring. To complete the effect, follow the decor you see here: Add a deep porcelain sink, open shelving for storage, butcher-block countertops, and an antique wood-burning stove. Pile the windowsills with a collection of shells or multicolored shards of broken pots. For bedrooms, hunt down old metal or brass bed frames and use simple cotton coverlets.

Or for the study in that widow's walk, introduce a simple, sturdy desk with lots of drawers and a hand-hooked rug to anchor it in the space. Visit an antique store for some old maps and photos of boats. Soon the look will come together, and you will have a place to think and dream about the sea.

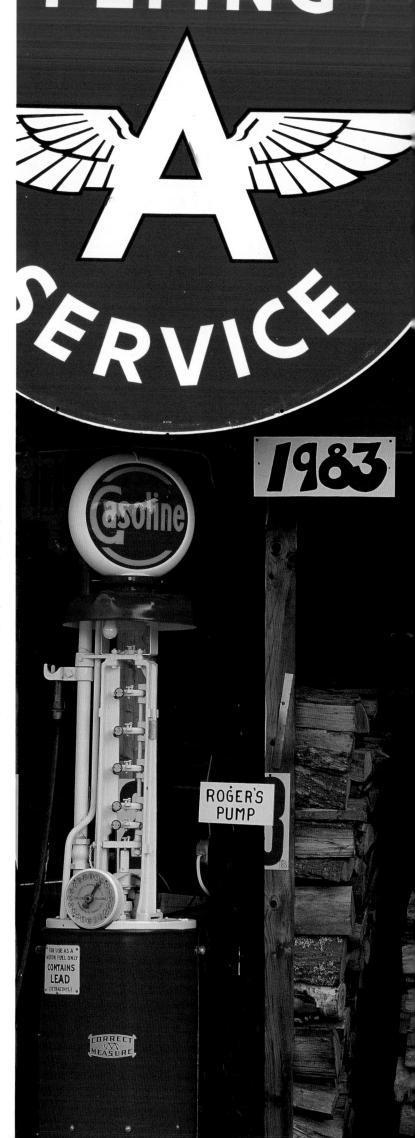

THE VINTAGE

Car Garage

There's nothing quite like packing a picnic and taking a summer drive on the back or secondary roads of New England. It's time to put top down and head for the open road. And it's not uncommon this season to see the impassioned lovers of antique cars out on the road, heading for a Fourth of July parade or a special meet. They may be members of the prestigious Antique Car Club of America. There are many ways to experience New England's style via car trip.

Some of the most beautiful country drives you will find here are on roads that lead to the region's vineyards. Spend a day, beginning in Massachusetts at Westport Rivers Vineyard and Winery and then head into Rhode Island to visit Greenvale Vineyard in Portsmouth, Newport Vineyards and Winery in Middletown, and Sakonnet Vineyards in Little Compton.

Tour Connecticut by following the roads to any one of the nine vineyards including:

*The Bishop Farms Winery, Cheshire

*Chamard Vineyards, Clinton

*DiGrazia Vineyards and Winery, Brookfield Center

*Haight Vineyard, Litchfield (The backroads here are all great drives.)

*Heritage Trail Vineyards, Lisbon

*Hopkins Vineyard, New Preston (Make sure you walk around this little town where the backdrop is waterfalls.)

*McLaughlin Vineyards, Sandy Hook

*Nutmeg Vineyard, Coventry (Take a break and visit Capriland's Herb Farm.)

*Stonington Vineyards, Stonington (Bring your camera or sketchbook to capture the interesting architecture.)

Take in New England's style with a road trip. You will go home with new ideas for living, designing, and planting.

If you take the shore route through Maine for a seaside tour, make a stop in York at the Parsons Family Winery. And if you go way north—not a bad thing in the summer—visit Bartlett Main Estate Winery in Gouldsboro or the Sow's Ear in Brooksville.

For a road tour with a literary theme head for Concord, Massachusetts, by way of Route 2. Go to Walden Pond, and then to the Concord Museum, which has the furnishings from Thoreau's cabin on Walden Pond and Ralph Waldo Emerson's study. In the same town is Orchard House, where Louisa May Alcott wrote *Little Women* and *Little Men*. From there you can head to Amherst to visit Emily Dickinson's homestead.

Or take a country drive on Route 7, starting in Cornwall, Connecticut, and make your destination the Robert Frost Museum in Shaftsbury. Frost lived at this farm on historic Route 7-A for several years, and it was here that he wrote "Stopping by the Woods on a Snowy Evening." The picturesque 1769 stone house sits on a treed lawn, and it is not hard to imagine how the place inspired Frost.

For a drive that focuses on the sea views and coastal villages, start in Kennebunk, Maine, and head north, hugging the coast through Portland, Boothbay, Camden, and Castine, all the way to Bar Harbor.

Another pretty shoreline route is Route 6-A in Sandwich, on Cape Cod. As you head south you will pass many antique shops, so the drive may be stop and go, depending on what catches your eye. You will find great lobster and clam shacks en route where you can dine with the top down and people-watch. Head all the way to Wellfleet and take a stroll through this small town, with its art galleries and interesting shopping.

Or follow the Connecticut shoreline starting in Guilford, and head west for Madison, Saybrook, Old Lyme, Mystic, and Stonington. All along the way you will see beautiful old homes—grand and not-so-grand, all studies in New England life. Plan your shoreline trips so you can visit a beach along the way. There is also great driving in Rhode Island through towns like Tiverton, Little Compton, and Sakonnet.

For drives that are steeped in history make your way to Old Sturbridge Village (Route 20), a study of nineteenth-century rural life, Old Deerfield off Route 5; or Plimoth Plantation in Plymouth, Massachusetts. Drive up to Livermore, Maine, to the Norlands Living History Center where you can learn about life in the eighteenth and nineteenth centuries through hands-on activities.

Another way to see the best of the country roads is to take off for a county fair. In Vermont there's the Bondsville Fair in Winhall; Champlain Valley Exposition in Essex Junction; and the Vermont State Fair, Rutland.

Summer is the perfect time to visit the region's historic mansions and gardens, and getting there often puts you on scenic roads in some of the prettiest towns. It is an interesting way to look at a number of things that embody New England style:

In New Bedford, Massachusetts, one of the old whaling towns, you can visit the Rotch-Jones-Duff House & Garden Museum. This is a whaling-era mansion built in 1834 and has a full city block of formal gardens.

In Gloucester, Massachusetts, the oceanside home of interior designer Henry Davis Sleeper, Beauport, is an amazing example of architect Stanford White's Shingle Style, and is augmented by the Fletcher Steele gardens. (Drive on Route 127 with the top down all the way! The ocean will be at your side, the breeze in your face.)

In the pretty town of Wiscasset, Maine, stands the 1807 mansion of Captain William Nickels with its own period gardens.

Sitting on a beautiful promontory that juts into Narragansett Bay and the open ocean, Newport, Rhode Island, has been a magnet for the wealthy since the 1700s. The city's oceanfront "cottages" are really mansions that have become studies in architecture, craftsmanship, and design. There is nothing like this anywhere else in New England. These homes were created in the Gilded Age by wealthy New Yorkers who took tax-free money and built these extravagant seaside spaces that ultimately defined them. Gold leaf, hand-carved marble—no expense was spared in design. Today, these spectacular reminders of a lifestyle most of us will never experience can be observed and visited. Many are the creations of architect Richard Morris Hunt, whose work recalls palaces of Europe. Some summer day visit one of them: Belcourt Castle, Rosecliff, The Breakers, Chateau-sur-Mer, Ocre Court, Marble House, The Elms, Beechwood, Kingsote, or Hammersmith Farm, where Jacqueline Kennedy Onassis (née Bouvier) grew up.

THE UNSPOILED CHATHAM

Beach Cottage

Sometimes we are lucky enough to find a place that is pure in its aging, a place where the stories of life come through in a knick or scratch, the way a doorknob rattles, or a window squeaks on the rise. Nothing really changes for years and years. The details like this, the sweet smell of old wood, the quilts as they rise from the cedar closet, seem to expand with time's passing. All this, which goes with living here, seems to talk to us of a season we love, a place we love to have. The smoothness of old porcelain sinks and knobs stops us sometimes and makes us think about all the big and little hands that turned them in maybe a hundred years. The hand-built cubbies and shelves have held glasses, seashell collections, and summer mystery novels. And the layers of paint that peek through a worn space speak of many a summer past.

This little house in Chatham is such a place. It is a dreamy, perfect New England house by the sea. When your car disappears behind the hedges of green, and you face the ocean and this faded little structure framed in blue, you can truly leave the world as you know it behind. When you enter the house, the old bead board walls wrap around you and the views to the open sea enchant. The familiar floor creaks or the ivy coming right up through the floor just takes you.

The owners found this house one day while walking through the neighborhood. When they peered in the windows, they fell in love with its simplicity, its pureness.

As the story goes, this was built as one of four homes—a main house and three small ones, one for each of a local man's daughters—of a family compound on a private oceanside point. This is the only one left of the three, and the 30-by-30-foot structure has barely changed since 1902. The second family to own the

cottage never did get around to renovating it. They just rebuilt the porch when it rotted out. Today this couple, the latest caretakers of this summer place, Lindsay Boutros-Ghali, her husband Adam Klein, and their new baby Georgia enjoy it just as it is. Its rawness is its charm, beauty, and the poetry of a place by the sea.

Open shelving in the kitchen, pans hung on nails, and a butcher block topping an old bureau to expand the workspace keeps the spirit of place. The built-in writing table hangs from a wall, installed to save space, and a great old closet with slanted shelves holds glassware. Nothing modern, with more space and better planning, can replace even these. And that isn't even a passing thought. Furniture sits in the background, milky white, perhaps so that it does not take away from views that change color with the light of day and the passing weather.

Honeysuckle, cedar, broom, and beach plum are plantings that add a little texture to the scenery—framing what could be the page of a 1903 Cape Cod calendar. Rosa Rugosa encircles a private place to sit near the water, a sanctuary of pink perfume. A place that lets you take in the sounds, sights, and smell of a summer day in its purest form.

New England's lakeside cottages and mountain camps, from Kezar Lake, Maine, to Wellfleet, Massachusetts, have special family places like this hidden around dark blue bends on the shoreline. They are places formed by summer rituals and recipes and passed along from visitor to visitor. They are places as individual as the people who come there, year after year, generation after generation.

The furnishings stay the same; they move only for the broom's swish and then they're back again. The

You can sit on this porch for hours on end and take in the view, the salty air, and bird songs of this time of year. This place gently moves you, like a friendly shove on the back of a swing, into its rhythm.

same checked blanket gets draped across the same couch. And so on. We like it this way. It comforts us.

How many of us recall that first walk to the strawberry patch, a bowl in one hand, Grandma's tight grasp in the other. Once home, we stopped up the sink for a cool berry wash, sugared the fruit, and then wrapped them like little red jewels in a blanket of buttery dough. From then on, every summer, we looked forward to that walk.

We remember, too, when the rain came down so hard we couldn't see past the screen porch. But we knew, like the summer before, we could pull the bed sheets off the bed and make a zigzag of tents with the rattan rocker and old wooden table. We didn't care about the rain. We loved the rat-a-tat-tat on the roof, and the way the sun always came out and made a smoky steam before us.

A game of checkers after dinner, and then a firefly-catching contest got us ready for bed. We carried our jars, flickering with their magical lights, off to our rooms, little summer candles we hoped would last the night.

If we close our eyes in the middle of winter, we can think of these summer places and smell them, too. Because the smells have come to us so many times, we have them in our grasp.

Pancakes on the griddle, when the butter starts a fast burn. Coffee that always brews too strong in the old pot Mom got with Green Stamps. That salty smell that whips up after a storm, or the muddy, wormy smell after a lakeside downpour. And the familiar smell of wet towels—so many in the bedroom, it gets a little muggy.

We love all of these summer house things. And no matter how old we get, we can always think back and see those fireflies, those nights when the shooting stars felt as though they'd hit us on the head, and the fizzling out of a wet fire.

These are summer places that make the season's change seem only a curtain coming down for Act II.

When dawn breaks and the sky is a watercolor wash of pink and powder blue, a low tide calm at your toes, going sailing can make you feel summer in your soul. That's the great thing about this season: the times of day are varied, dramatic, and compelling. As the sun comes to mid-day, her heat releases a sweet perfume scent from the island sea grass. A summer breeze carries the scent to everyone, another bookmark of the perfect day. Don't miss these moments in New England. Make sure you feel this season on an island, whether it's tiny Swan's Island, or Islesboro in Maine or the collection of Thimble Islands off the Connecticut shore. Bring your sail down, and hold the moment.

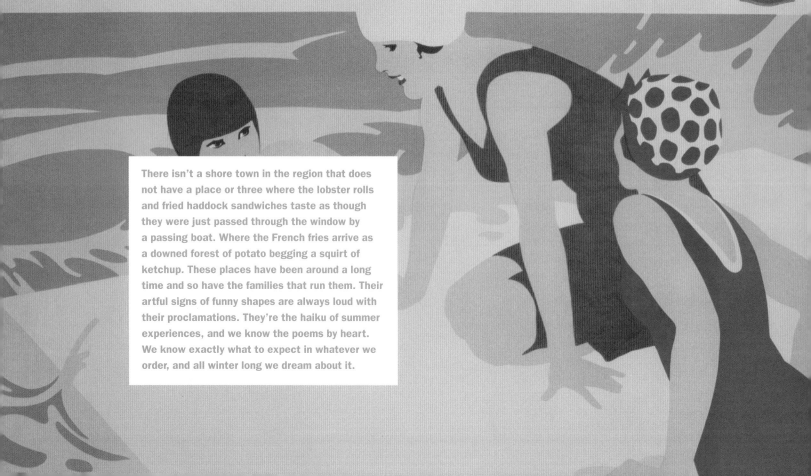

There isn't a shore town in the region that does not have a place or three where the lobster rolls and fried haddock sandwiches taste as though they were just passed through the window by a passing boat. Where the French fries arrive as a downed forest of potato begging a squirt of ketchup. These places have been around a long time and so have the families that run them. Their artful signs of funny shapes are always loud with their proclamations. They're the haiku of summer experiences, and we know the poems by heart. We know exactly what to expect in whatever we order, and all winter long we dream about it.

Fall

By the end of August in New England, an early-morning walk offers subtle but familiar hints that fall is coming. A tree we've passed all summer long suddenly has a fiery red leaf peeking through the green. And as time passes, the hardy marigold goes from sunny yellow to brown after a few mild icings of frost. We harvest and bag our seeds; we can our fruit. Our once-lush gardens quietly wither and bend with each cooler day. By the time the pumpkins show their weight across the fields, our landscape is awash in fall colors. We pack up our beach bags, silence the sun umbrella with a tight twist and snap, and begin the climb to the attic where our days of sand, sunscreen, and barbecues are tucked away to wait silently for spring. We carry the palette of this new season indoors so that the loss of sun and light is minimized. Harvested apples piled high in painted pottery make the perfect centerpiece for our dinner tables. The pumpkin—carved with a smile, hollowed for candlelight—adorns our door with a cornstalk and waits to greet goblins and ghosts who will visit shortly, sticky hands and all, rattling the door for treats. Our pantry shelves are lined with a rainbow of glass jars, the fruits of our garden labor—deep-purple beets, fire-engine red tomatoes, strawberry jams, and blueberry jellies. Bike rides, flea markets, hikes, and country drives replace our days at the beach. It is a time when we bring things into our nests for comfort and inspiration. We check the wood bin, happy to feel the papery lightness of the logs. And when it's time to open the flue, strike the match, and move to the hearth, we know the next season is being clocked, each fire a tick and tock to winter.

THE IPSWICH

Antique Home

Drive through any New England town, whether it's Camden, Maine, or Ipswich, Massachusetts, and the antique home will become a familiar sight. Such homes are bordered in hand-placed stone walls that are painstakingly fitted stone by stone, with much thought to the materials' color, size, and shape. Some of these walls trail into the woods, seamlessly blending into the landscape. Others are circled by pristine white picket fences, their backyard gardens punctuated with arborways woven in heirloom roses.

Those who settle here embrace and honor the past. The farmhouse. The sea captain's house topped by a widow's walk. The grand old mansion. Their current owners are careful not to disturb the work that brought the historic structures into being. This passion for craftsmanship filters through the details that fill these homes—the collectibles that sit on the tabletops, and line the windowsills, and the woven creations that lie underfoot.

We honor the builders and the families of these special places with plaques that confirm their presence and hand. Even though modern life has dovetailed with these architectural gems, their wide pine floors, horsehair plaster walls, and beamed ceilings frequently remain intact as we, the modern-day caretakers, ever so carefully work to restore and keep them. Interiors are often designed in ways that remind us of those bygone days. New Englanders work with craftsmen who know authentic restorative techniques, and then they hunt for those design details—the old captain's mirror, the hand-sewn patchwork quilt, the needlepoint rug—

that reveal, when we enter these rooms, that time has stood still.

Everything—the houses, their art and furnishings—get recycled in time, and the region's antique stores, auctions, barn sales, and outdoor flea markets are the lifeblood of this process. It is the fall that brings the antique sales and the hunters together.

In Search of Antiques and Fall Scenes
North of Boston, Old Town Marblehead is a tangle of streets and a jumble of colonial-era houses, bookstores, and antique stores, all within a block of the harbor.

In Salem, a few minutes north, the Salem Common, Chestnut Street, Derby Square, and Essex Street will give you a good dose of striking architecture. As you wander about, notice the antique stores sandwiched in between.

All along Route 1-A, heading north from Beverly to Newburyport, old homes and antique stores line the way. Depending on the town, there may be five or forty antique sellers.

Head for Essex, a right onto Route 133, and you will be in "antique alley." Break from the hunt with a stop at Woodman's, Farnhams, or the Village Restaurant for the best lobster and clams you'll find in the state.

Continuing on Route 1-A will land you in Rowley, where the Todd Farm will tempt you to continue your antique hunt. Five minutes from here you can get a great piece of banana cream pie or a meatloaf lunch at the Agawam Diner—a place that's had lines out the door for more than twenty-five years.

Antique houses like this one
tell a story about a town's or a
village's beginnings. The detail,
or lack thereof, speaks to a
slice of New England history.
From the grand sea captain's
houses of Newburyport
and Salem to the simple farmhouse, we can trace life here.

With heirlooms, auctions, and antique stores, New Englanders can stop time in their rooms. And when their front doors close, they can really leave the day behind.

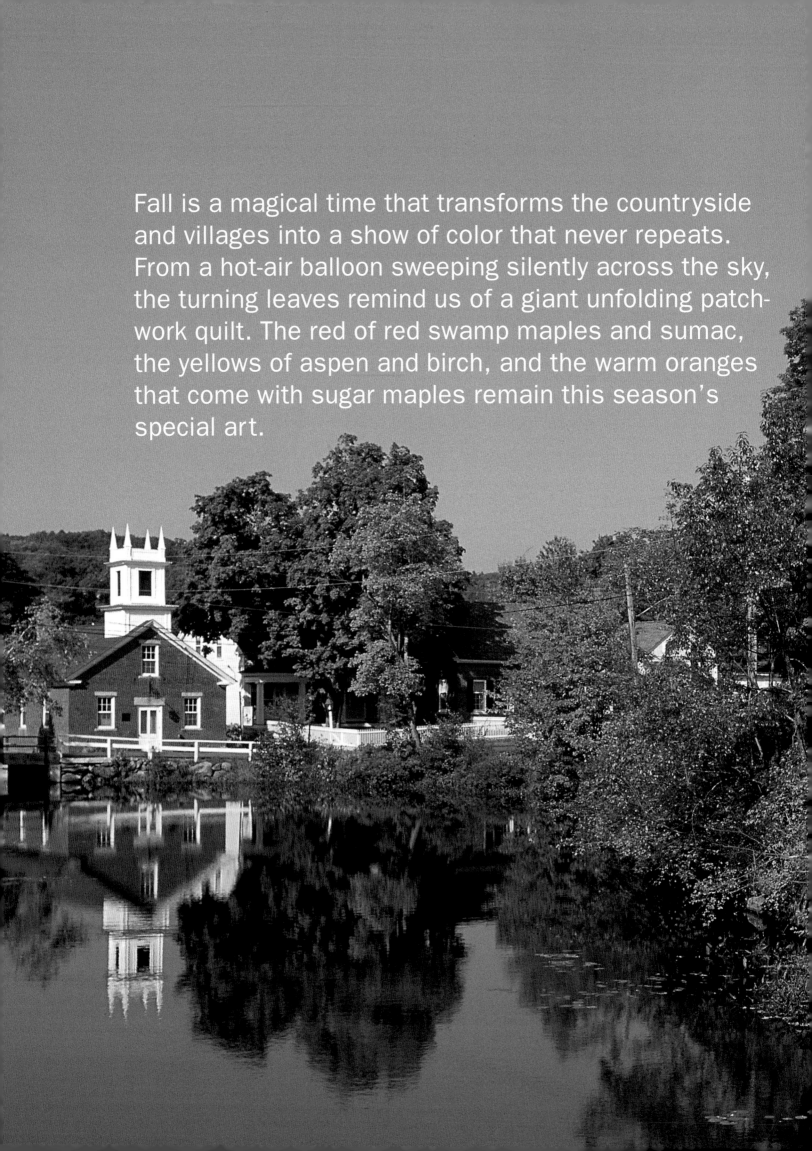

Fall is a magical time that transforms the countryside and villages into a show of color that never repeats. From a hot-air balloon sweeping silently across the sky, the turning leaves remind us of a giant unfolding patchwork quilt. The red of red swamp maples and sumac, the yellows of aspen and birch, and the warm oranges that come with sugar maples remain this season's special art.

We like to hold moments of the past in our view; touch what others have crafted, sat on, studied, and worked with. That sense of time and place—and past generations—gives New England a plethora of romantic textures. And so, when on a fall drive we pass that barn sale, the car wheel turns so naturally as we sigh at the thought of the new view from bed or hearth that we will create.

Perhaps it was Grandma's old apron, the one that hung on the drawer pull at the beach house. The paisley one she wore when she baked peach cobbler. Maybe it was the first blanket on which the baby slept or the flag we raised each Fourth of July at the Nantucket cottage. These little snippets of our life's movies are held in fabric scrapbooks called quilts. They make their way to porch chairs and overstuffed couches, the icing on the cake of our comfort zones.

THE NEW HAMPSHIRE

Original

When you wake up in a three-hundred-year-old home with its original glass windows, you see the morning light differently. And the view out is different, too. The fields or pond in the distance, framed in hand-sawn casings and sun-bleached sills, look somehow more picturesque than if your eyes peered through new windows. Old wood sills smell sweet when the sun warms them. The floorboards, polished with a beeswax finish, are incomparable to any modern substitute. The day to come—though perhaps in a busy, high-tech world—is far away.

There is a lot of feedback in an old house. Wide pine floors may have handmade nails threaded across the boards that look like top hats. They've risen over time, as the ground has moved and reshaped the house, and they greet or snag a passing woolen sock. Front and back stairways have their distinctive creaks as you move about. Somehow you memorize those sounds without even realizing it, so when someone's little feet pad about, you know just where they're off to. The kitchen fireplace that you have come to know may need logs piled higher than the living room's hearth. And as the seasons change from fall to winter, each room takes on a heightened personality. You have to remember to put the draft stopper between the library and the baby's room. The third rock from the left on the stone wall will need a little adjusting before the snow comes. It always falls. You just know that.

Timepieces like this antique home sit quietly, tucked into the landscape, all over the region. The wise builders of the era never competed with Mother Nature's rolling green or wood. They worked to fit homes in like puzzle pieces.

But that is what New Englanders cherish. Homes with character. Homes with special personalities. They are more than shelter. They are our old friends. Some are quirky. Some are truly odd. Many are haunted. There are stories of sad ghosts who leave a chill in the air as they move through the halls looking for a loved one. Or stories of ghosts who wail once a year on the anniversary of their child's death. We live among them, respect them, and let them be.

Many houses in New England have hiding rooms for runaway slaves, birthing rooms that allowed only women and the town doctor, below-ground kitchens for the maids and butlers, or tiny servants' quarters tucked into the rafters or behind the kitchen of grander homes. And there are many New England homes with their share of hidden stairways that kept the movement of domestic help out of the owners' view.

When we move to these special places, our modern life in tow, we work hard to hold on to the stories of the places—passing them on to family members and friends as they come and go.

We look to nature and the changing New England seasons to cue our palettes inside and out. Being understated and true to the style of the period of our homes gives us the best of both worlds we live in.

We look to the hills and dales for inspiration. A staircase may recall a wooded path at dusk, a stenciled wall reminds us that spring's coming . . . and our porch reflects the simplicity of the landscape.

Travel the region's towns and villages and you will come across the creative forces of potters, wool spinners, and candlestick makers. They're tucked into towns where tradition is cherished and celebrated—where the Fourth of July parade brings out all the townspeople. The muskets are shined, the flags hand-pressed, and the band practices year-round for special celebrations. And there are people who live our history and traditions at Sturbridge Village and Plimoth Plantation, passing the ways of the past on to others.

When the last car door slams shut and we head
down the dirt path for the apple orchard, our
nostrils fill with that familiar sweet, ripe smell.
Ahead lie the neat rows of trees, red and green
against a perfect blue sky. The only sound is
that of bees buzzing.

As we move through the foliage in search of our
bounty, the sun ticks across the sky, taking this
sweet fall day away. Soon our kitchen sinks will
be filled with these luscious fruits, ready to be
transformed into fritters, scones, pies, and tarts.

Apples mark a special season's time in New
England. They bring a host of activities that will
hold us in our kitchens through winter.

CIDER

"apple a day"

APPLES

THE BOSTON

Townhouse

From Boston's Prudential Center or the John Hancock observatory, you can look down at the city's neighborhoods and the sea of red brick that shapes each—the North End, the South End, Beacon Hill, the Back Bay, and the Fenway. Just think, every brick began in the palm of someone's hand and was placed, fitted, and cemented into each of these architectural gems. Walk the streets of Boston, and your soles touch where history has been made, where great men have walked. A world-class city steeped in historic significance, Boston continues to be home to events and people known the world over. It carries the common thread of New England style in its architecture, gardens, and traditions. But it's a city of contrasts, in its people and its style.

Every section is its own, unique experience. The North End, a winding jumble of little streets that wrap the waterfront, offers every Italian delicacy imaginable from its restaurants, bakeries, and storefronts, all sandwiched between residences—including Paul Revere's house.

Walk to the waterfront warehouses-turned-shopping-oasis, Quincy Market, with the ocean to your back, and eventually you will bump into Beacon Hill, the oldest neighborhood in the city. Brick houses line the Hill's narrow streets, and a plethora of secret gardens hide behind wooden doors and brick walls. They are peaceful sanctuaries that muffle the city's din, bring the birds to feeders, and add color and texture to the views, inside to out.

At Pinkney and Mount Vernon is Louisberg Square, where two grand brick ribbons of homes face each other, with a lick of green park between. At one time Louisa May Alcott lived here, as did novelist William Dean Howells. Louisberg Square's current residents include an impressive mix of the very rich and the very famous.

Gas lit lamps and cobblestone paths are as common as the politicians heading for the gold-domed State House that sits at the very top of the Boston Common. The 1798 Charles Bulfinch creation perches above the forty-five acres of grass and paved walkways. Historically a pasture, hanging ground for thieves, a military post, and even a place to duel, the Boston Common functions now as an island of green for walking commuters, neighborhood baseball games, winter skating, and water games at Frog Pond. Concerts and fairs reserve space here as well. It's a great place to survey the surroundings—from the antiquarian bookshops on nearby Boylston Street to the new, sleek Ritz-Carlton.

Just a few steps across Charles Street from the Common is the Public Garden where in spring and summer the red and green swan boats glide across the pond carrying giggling children through the water playground of the swans and ducks. Old weeping willows hug the shore, their tufts of branch sway in and out of the water like elegant matrons tossing their locks to and fro. Beds of flowers, winding paths punctuated by trees from around the world, and statues honoring great men give the surrounding homes the most sought-after views and real estate in the city—with, of course, the highest prices.

Residents of the Hill, the Back Bay, and the area off the Commonwealth Avenue Mall—where even grander, larger single-family homes once were in great number—stroll with their pups, shop, and dine on Charles, Boylston, and Newbury Streets. A little longer walk to the South End, minutes from Copley Square, takes them to the trendy new eateries, galleries, and shops that have been popping up in the past five years.

Narrow little Charles Street has the highest concentration of antique stores woven in and around to what is called the Flats, or the base of Beacon Hill. They come in all sizes and shapes and each has its own personality and offerings. There are specialty shops that sell everything from kitchen supplies to stationery, and cozy eateries and town houses turned inn.

For groceries or ingredients for a picnic in the Public Garden or along the Charles River, visit De Luca's, a family-owned grocery that's a fixture here. The striped awning and seasonal cues like pumpkins and firewood make this hard to miss or pass by.

Stroll from the Public Garden to the Commonwealth Avenue Mall, which stretches from Arlington Street to Massachusetts Avenue, and you will pass many townhouses and mansions. Tucked behind those big front doors with brass knockers are hundreds of homes born of the breakup of one-time single-family homes. Old Boston families—and new—are the fiber of the place. In mansions turned condominiums, interiors hold the old detail, while design taste swings from pure antiques to contemporary mixed with a little retro, and beyond. Head to the South End and see where artists have converted warehouses into condos, bringing industrial buildings to new, eclectic highs.

The different roof lines and architectural details—from gargoyles to lush window boxes, wisteria-wrapped brick walls, and clematis vines unfurling to the ground—make a walk through downtown a fireworks display of stimuli.

One block away from Commonwealth Avenue is Newbury Street, which starts at the Public Garden and the old Ritz-Carlton Hotel and Residences. Here, on this comfortably scaled street of galleries, cafes, spas and hair salons, a whole new energy vibrates. Jutting from behind the rooftops are Boylston Street's highrises—a contrast in a visual time machine. It's said there are more than one hundred hair salons here, and they've all managed to stay in business for a long time. The stretch ends at Massachusetts Avenue, where funkier stores cater to the college town's clientele.

Take a right onto Massachusetts Avenue, cross the bridge over the Charles, and, as many Back Bay residents say, you enter the world of Cambridge. This will take you right to Harvard University and all there is to discover in and about Harvard Square, from bookstores to cafes of every ethnic pleasure.

While Boston holds a grand collection of renowned universities, medical centers, museums, restaurants, music halls, and theaters (and is the home of the Red Sox!), it is a city that invites you to meander on foot. It's the best way to take in the history that is so evident at every turn.

Harvard. Great men and women have walked
these same paths for generations. Movies have
been made here. More importantly, lives and
discoveries have. It's a place everyone should
walk, and take in.

THE MAINE

Lakeside Retreat

There is nothing quite like waking up lakeside in a cabin in the fall. Maine's Sebego, Kezar, or Moosehead lakes are all great places to experience the season. These are places where you can just watch a day begin and end, a book and a thermos of coffee by your side.

On many mornings at this time of year, the lake water is warmer than the air and a dreamy, gauzy fog hangs low over the water. The fog will slowly blow off to the water's edges as you finish your morning coffee. The silence here, broken only by the cry of the loon or the whipping of a fly rod, feels right.

The lake water, absent of the motorboat, is a velvety smooth fabric that swells and levels and is crystal clear this far north. Stand at the shore and you can see silvery trout making their way past the sandy bottoms, sunlight piercing to the patchwork of color formed from fallen leaves.

We head for these peaceful places—the log cabin, the simple cottage (circa 1950s), the old resort— to escape the suit, the cell phone, and all that our complex, hurried lives hand us. The keepers of these simple places, sanctuaries for the worn and the weary, purposefully maintain their casual ease. It's been this way for over a hundred years. In fact, this region was a stylish escape in the 1800s. People came here then, as they do now, from the city to hide and decompress.

New England has an abundance of these lakeside retreats, places with wonderful traditions. They revolve around simple things—the outdoor grill, the canoe trip to an offshore island, a game of croquet, reading a yellowed, curled paperback from the communal library, and the faded thousand-piece puzzle everyone works on by the fire.

At some old camps or small resorts, the family-style meals in the lodge are a tradition. The start-your-day menus are all about comfort foods like biscuits, home fries, blueberry pancakes, and homemade jam. For the rest of the day, count on hearty New England meals of chowders, stews, and roasted meats. These are the places where the beds creak and handmade quilts keep them warm. Some haven't changed in more than fifty years. If there is a television, it's probably from the 1960s. The phone has a rotary dial, and the side table is covered in tacked linoleum.

Leave your cabin, walk the periphery of the lake, and take in the fall air, the blue sky, and the quiet. The only thing on your calendar is a canoe ride.

Maine's Birches Resort is in a picturesque birch grove overlooking Mount Kineo. Visitors stay in hand-hewn log cabins along the lake, with porches to catch great views. Wood-burning fireplaces or Franklin stoves keep you cozy when there's a chill in the air. The Migis Lodge in South Casco, on Sebago Lake, offers some thirty cottages on ninety-seven acres and canoes and sailboats for you to cruise this beautiful pool of blue.

But it doesn't matter whether you take a boat out or sit on the porch with a crossword puzzle till the sky turns red and the grills get lit. If you do head out to a little offshore island after dinner, bring a blanket and watch the stars come out, or take to a porch hammock and wait for a shooting-star show. It's so clear up here, you'll feel like they're going to rain down on you.

Moosehead Lake, in Maine's North Woods, is forty miles long with 320 miles of shoreline, so there's plenty of scenery—from birds to moose—on a fall day. You can take the water on any way you like—by canoe or sailboat, by rafting and kayaking, or from the shore. For a water adventure, take a boat up the Kennebec River to Moose River to Moosehead Lake then to Greenville. From there, floatplanes can take you to one of a choice of sporting camps.

If you'd like a look at this magnificent place from up high, you can hike Mount Katahdin or Mount Kineo. The latter is a shorter and faster journey with breathtaking views of the foliage below from a 750-foot-high cliff. Or, take an easy three-mile trek to the summit of Borestone Mountain right to the sanctuary, where you have a 360-degree view.

Here is a place where New England's best shines through. Fall's wash of color reflects perfectly in the lake waters, and when a canoe cuts through the satiny calm, the ripples that echo about take your breath away.

From the old lakeside resorts
to the farmhouses, we
New Englanders cherish our
structures and the things within
them. We like to take out
the same porch chair each year
and turn it to the same view
we've always had.

THE TOWN'S

Main Street

Many of the main streets in New England's villages and towns look much the way they did a hundred years ago, thanks to the passionate residents involved with preservation and historical groups. We New Englanders love our white clapboard and shuttered homes, the small scale of our main streets, and the history that unfolds with each turn in the road. The people who settle here as homeowners and shopkeepers come to take part in and contribute to this small-town life—from the Saturday-night bean suppers to town-wide Halloween festivities.

Everyone pretty much knows each other, and there is a sense of community that residents cherish. You'll even find city transplants who have come to follow their heart on a new creative venture, such as the two Boston lawyers who ran off to Swan's Island, Maine, and started Swan's Island Blankets. There are probably five stories like this for every village. They attract all kinds of people and businesses, holding on to businesses for generations. There are diners, department stores, and barbers—anchors that have been family businesses for more than forty years. Even those who are new to the towns have a genuine interest in what they offer. They are not here just to make a living. They are here to hold on to a lifestyle. Just as their storefronts are one-of-a-kind former stables turned stores or feed store turned gallery—so are their offerings. These places draw in the entrepreneurs who handpick or make their goods. And the inns and guesthouses are just as individual in their New England style.

The typical New England main street is a great mix of stores, from bakeries and galleries to antique shops, cafes, diners, and bookshops. Bookstores in these villages are almost as great a place to mingle with townspeople as the diner or general store. There are so many of them that you could take a driving tour through the region just to see them. In fact, it's rare to find a town that doesn't have at least one, if not two, bookstores—one for new titles and one for used or antiquarian finds. And while running into a store to get an errand done is efficient, it's not what happens to townsfolk. Going into the village bakery or hardware store gets you in a conversation with townspeople. You find out when the orchard starts baking pies. It slows you down, lets you feel the day. And with time, it grows on you and you become part of it.

Postcard-perfect, the villages and small towns celebrate and announce the seasons and holidays at their doors. Pumpkins, scarecrows, and hay bales appear as Halloween gets closer on the calendar. Christmas wreaths and trees follow, cueing a new season. Daffodils and lush spring planters adorn storefronts as the warm weather season arrives. And up and down main street, the homeowners join in, keeping the traditions of the town at their doors.

If you decide to tour New England, stay off the highways and take every scenic route you can. They're well worth it. You won't want to miss the scenery or those special places the guidebooks don't talk about.

Go to seaside towns like Castine, Camden, or Kennebunkport, Maine, or Manchester-by-the-Sea, Pride's Crossing, Newburyport, and Rockport, Massachusetts. Contrast those to the Connecticut villages of Salisbury, Woodbury, Kent, Essex, Chester, and Stonington. Move on to Tiverton, Rhode Island, and then Newport. Save Dorset, Woodstock, and Manchester, Vermont, for Christmas time. And do not miss the lakes and mountain regions of New Hampshire in summer. No town or village looks like another, and no main street store is ever duplicated.

The architecture, landscape, and period gardens will deplete your supply of film, pastels, or paints. Your journal will fill with observations, lists of revisits, and maybe even where you want to settle down someday.

Much of the inspiration for our homes connects to the seasons, landscape, and character of New England's villages.

ENGINE COMPANY
—No. 6—

NORWICH
FIRE DEPT.

Kief's
BARBER SHOP
AND MEN'S HAIR STYLING

BARBER SHOP

OPEN

LONGLEY

I WANT YOU
TO GET A HAIRCUT

SHOE STORE IN AMERICA

LBURN SHOE STORE

PAINTS

Coca-Cola
Delicious and Refreshing

Tips
Dark Harbor

ALISSON'S
RESTAURANT

OPEN

Woods
COIN LAUNDRY

Come
The
will
your

THE VERMONT

General Store

Drive through New England and chances are, one of the things you'll pass by is the general store. Vermont, though, just might have most of them. Often they're big, boxy old structures with signs that can stretch across the width of the building. Step inside and listen up, and you'll learn about the locals and life in their village. And except for the modern products on the shelves, many look like they did in the 1800s.

The Craftsbury General Store in Craftsbury, Vermont, is typical. In the days when snow came up past your knees and the horses couldn't pull the buggy past the barn, having one store in the village was a godsend. People shopped the general stores for everything, from chicken feed and far-fresh eggs to shovels and saws. Today you can still get all of that, but you'll also find the stuff of contemporary life: a video selection, dog biscuits, fresh bait, maybe even a gourmet to-go lunch. Each store has its own personality, and some are more successful in remaining authentic in spirit.

The Vermont Country Store of Weston was founded by Vrest and Ellen Orton in 1946. Running a country store was in Vrest's blood; his dad, Gardener, opened his own general store in 1897. At Vrest and Ellen's store or in their catalog, you can find things you thought were obsolete. The catalog entices buyers to consider a "furniture-quality" cabinet holding a turntable for 33 $1/3$, 45, and 78 rpm records with the headline "Strike Up the Band and Bring Your Favorite Music to Life with Our 3-Speed Record Player." Then there's Lifebuoy soap, in case you missed it growing up, the "world's first deodorant soap, with its original bright-red color and distinctive fragrance." Just perusing their catalog turns back the clock.

Some general store owners still live upstairs or out back, so they can get to the kitchen before dawn to bake, prep food, and stock the shelves. Locals still come to the country store to stock up on town news as well as supplies. Who died, who was born, who got divorced, and who is sick and needs some help with chores is the news that's filled the aisles since the day the stors opened. This neighborly connection is the fiber of small-town life and the quality people continue to crave and hold on to despite the sea of strip malls that pop up.

In the quaint little town of Dorset, Vermont, Peltier's Market sits on the town green like a big, worn-in chair, inviting you to come in and spend time. It's a pretty irresistible place. You have to climb big, wide wood steps and swing open the door to enter. Like the perfect postcard, it is one of a few old clapboard public buildings encircling the green, along with the Dorset Inn, the post office, and an art gallery. It's been here since 1816, making it one of the oldest country stores in the United States. Not long ago it was rated "The Best of the Best Country Stores" by *Vermont* magazine. Jay Hathaway, who owns it today, is quick to tell you he loves the business, the town, and his customers. Peltier's is the kind of place that has everything you need to survive: fresh baked goods, a good wine selection, dry goods, and people who can make your day better. Village life and country stores are connected by the people who come and go throughout the day, generation after generation.

Each general store has its own twist. Store to store, aisle to aisle, you can tour the state, going from one to another, always discovering new things to look at, eat, or wear. At the Country Store in Montpelier, opened in 1850, you can find gourmet and specialty foods, many of which come from Vermont, such as Champlain Chocolates and Green Mountain Coffee Roasters coffee. The Country Store's motto perhaps summarizes the view that it likely inspires in others: "We sell products that don't come back, to people who do."

Come stay awhile. Catch up on the news of the day. Pick up a homemade sandwich. And don't forget the milk. This is the essence of the general store.

With winter's white blanket ready to fall across our fields, it seems so fitting that fall gives us one last burst of dramatic color on the countryside. The sky is vivid blue, the sun so bright. The shadows beneath our feet are deep and dark. When the pumpkins finally mature in the fields, it looks as though we've had a magical beach-ball rain shower. Stop by a farm and pick your own for carving. There's nothing quite like cutting one from its vine and giving it a home on your front stoop, where it can light the way for a few Halloween goblins. Find the perfect one on a country drive some weekend in Grafton, Vermont, New Preston, Connecticut, or Dublin, New Hampshire.

HOMEMADE

On the Farm

It doesn't get more New England than the big red barn. These architectural jewels symbolize the down-to-earth spirit that is a farmer's life. All over the region many farms are still family-owned; often, they set up produce stands that bring us everything from fresh arugula to asparagus and corn.

Farms in every state open their barn doors or set up roadside stands offering whatever they grow, bake, or create in cheese caves and kitchens. Drive through Enfield, Connecticut, and stop in at Trinity Farm, where four generations of the Smyth family have been in the dairy business. Today Michael Smyth is delivering milk door to door, just as his dad Tom did when Michael was a little boy. The farm is right next door to the big old white clapboard house where he and his four siblings grew up. His mom, Betty, and his dad still live there. Michael, his wife, Dale, their children, and now their grandchildren work on the farm. Raw and pasteurized milk, homemade yogurt, fresh eggs, and cream are available daily. Homemade ice cream is on their "to do" list.

The Smyths' farm is no different from many family-owned farms in New England, all of which bring the locals fresh food sans the middleman, and with lots of heart. Goodale Orchards in Ipswich, Massachusetts, has lines out its barn door during apple-picking season. Locals come in for fresh herbs, vegetables, and cider. And when the apple cider doughnuts or the apple pies are coming off the stove, many a person's willpower collapses.

New Englanders tend to keep
time in check with collections
and furnishings that are, if not
authentic, relevant to the
land. But the region is chock-
full of furniture-makers who
can duplicate pieces from just
about any period.

In typical New England fashion, we don't like to bulldoze the abandoned farms. We cherish these wonderful old timepieces. In fact, it's become quite fashionable to live in a converted or rebuilt barn. Some builders, like David Lanoue in Stockbridge, Massachusetts, have barn inventory for anyone who wants an old barn to call home. Lanoue and his crew carefully take barns down piece by piece and store them until they're called upon for a new life. The barns' open layout, interesting shapes, and historic significance are attracting a new breed of homeowner—one who is preserving New England's special landscape.

To experience life on a farm without owning one, you can stay at one of many working farm inns in the region. Perhaps one of the most spectacular is Shelburne Farms in Vermont. The Inn at Shelburne Farms, a Queen Anne Revival manor house that dates to 1889, is just up the hill.

A national historic site, this 1,400-acre working farm in Vermont's Lake Champlain Valley was originally the model farm and agricultural estate of William Seward and Lila Vanderbilt Webb. What is now the inn was once their home. Today the farm is a nonprofit educational organization devoted to preserving and adapting its historic buildings and landscape for teaching and demonstrating the stewardship of natural and agricultural resources.

Children can milk a cow, touch the farm animals, collect eggs, and see how farmhouse cheddar cheese is made from the milk of the herd of Brown Swiss cows.

At Berkson Farms in Enosburg Falls, Vermont, guests can feed the animals, collect eggs, brush and pet the donkey, milk, hay, or help with barn chores.

The Inn at Mountain View Creamery in East Burke, Vermont, was built in 1883 by Elmer A. Darling, who trained in architecture at M.I.T. and built a series of interesting barns around a courtyard. The cow barn, measuring 300 feet long, is one of the largest structures in the state and is a landmark for students of design and history. There are all kinds of farm animals here, as well as organic vegetable and perennial gardens, and 440 acres for visitors to meander around.

When you and your horse leave the barn at a slow gallop, headed for the woods—hooves crunching down on fall leaves, the smell of leather and boot polish in the air—nothing else seems to matter. And except for maybe a horse-drawn sleigh ride, there is no better way to feel the season and experience New England's hills and dales. There are stables in every state and horses for every level of experience. You can stay at inns that feature horseback riding, and you can even take an inn-to-inn horse-riding tour in Vermont. The Kendron Valley Inn in South Woodstock, Vermont, has stables and tours on horseback. If you prefer to watch horses, there's the Myopia Hunt Club in Hamilton, Massachusetts, and the Quechee Vermont Polo Club in Quechee, Vermont.

ALL HORSES

Winter

When you look out your window and watch the first snow of the season, you feel as though you are in one of those little plastic Woolworth's domes that, when shaken, brings the flakes in a fury. Sometimes it comes when there is no bitter wind. The storm of white descends instead when the temperature just slips to thirty-two degrees, and we can imagine that magical moment when the raindrops somehow collide and collect on the way down to form those fat and lofty flakes. They stick to the porch furniture, the top of the stone wall, and the edge of our tree branches—decorating everything they touch as though the snow chefs were furiously practicing their piping techniques. The light changes this season. The landscape takes on more purple as dusk falls. We have more dark days and find ourselves craving the warm sun we had gotten so used to. Burnt-orange and yellow parkas, multicolored ski scenes on our sweaters and blankets, and rich, warm patterns that come to our rooms ease us into, and sustain us in, this season of white. It is a time to come together inside to nest. Our dormant kitchens come back to life. The barren fireplace is ready for the strike of the match.

A CHEF'S

Winter Kitchen

The quintessential New England farmhouse is a white clapboard structure in a setting that includes apple trees, maple trees for syrup, a vegetable garden, kitchen cutting garden, and some hive boxes for honey. Having a happy cow giving rich milk that we can turn into butter or ice cream, some chickens and geese for eggs, and maybe a few sheep for wool completes the farm. With all of this focus on food, the kitchen is one of the most important rooms in a farmhouse. It is where the family comes together to work with its harvest—to wash the produce or fresh eggs, to cook, share thoughts on the day, and eventually eat together. These aren't fancy places. They are warm, colorful, and textural. It is where the basil, thyme, and rosemary come straight from the garden and are tied with a cotton string and hung to dry in a corner, where tomatoes line the windowsill for a last ripening, and fresh eggs are piled high in Grandma's old crockery bowl. The only thing with a big shine may be the pie, whose crust is lacquered with egg whites.

We New Englanders like to bookmark our kitchens with furnishings, kitchen tools, and vessels that have followed us from childhood or were passed down through the family. There is nothing better than looking up a yellow-cake recipe in a family cookbook, the corners of the page a little stained. We like to turn the fritters with Mom's wooden spoon or cork the wine with Dad's old brass-topped stopper. This is a kitchen that embraces materials that work to suit our purposes, look better as time passes, and are made sometimes of things with local roots.

Cook's Illustrated publisher Christopher Kimball has a Vermont farmhouse that blends old and new, cap-turing the spirit and qualities of the region by combining nostalgia and utility. The inspiration for his kitchen came from his days as a young boy summering in the area; the yellow farmhouse of a family friend and town baker, Marie Briggs, was just down the road. Today Chris, his wife Adrienne, and their brood of four enjoy every inch of this kitchen, a place created to accommo-date the eight little hands mixing dough, sugaring berries, or stirring soup on a winter's day.

Just off the back of the kitchen is a walk-in pantry that holds kitchen tools, as well as the Kimball family's bottled honey gathered from their beehives and maple syrup tapped from some one hundred trees on the property.

The countertops and sink are made of soapstone, a material that nicks and scratches—over time, a deep gash here or there will recall a great day or a disaster in the kitchen. Like a scrapbook of kitchen life, it holds the history of the room rather than washing it away with a swish of a sponge on slick granite.

There are three stoves here. Two sit on brick floors and are backed in brick as well. No worrying over spilled milk or burned apple-pie filling. Chris uses the antique wood-burning stove to bake bread and maybe slow-cook a winter stew. There's a workhorse Viking, as well as an Aga in yet another kitchen room. He loves his 1920s refrigerator as much as his modern one. And with a root cellar nearby, there doesn't seem to be anything lacking in this farmhouse kitchen. A big work-table sits in the center of the floor, covered in Vermont marble, offering up enough space to roll pastry on one end and cut up apples at the other.

The pantry is the perfect place
to store the bounty of the farm.
Open shelving keeps the
guesswork out of where things
are, and homemade labels,
simple glass storage jars,
and crockery keep it non-fussy
and functional in true New
England style.

Somehow it is fitting to make bread in a wood-burning stove in winter. The whole kitchen gets warmed up, and the sweet smell of wood merging with the forming of a bread crust keeps us feeling cozy...loving what a winter day can bring.

This antique stove is a perfect fit for a simmering stew and bread baking.

If you meander along the back roads of New England, you might pass trees marked as maple syrup producers by the attached tin buckets. And it's not just maple syrup that will come from this tapping. Maple candy and butter originate here as well. Maple syrups are graded, like fine wines, from light to dark, and you might just distinguish unique qualities if you compare one state's to another, like Maine and Vermont. You can buy fresh syrup right from a farm stand or the village country store.

SOUTH FACE FARM

THE CHRISTMAS

Tree Farm

One of the best things about Christmas in New England is the way its landscape and traditions nourish our imaginations. Think about the last time you watched the snowflakes come down like rain—and how they sat on your sleeve, glued down like sequined stars. Or the last time they came past your face so fast you breathed them in, feathery little shapes that wet your cool cheeks. It's the snow that stops us and signals that Christmas is not far. It says it may be time to get to the Christmas tree farm. It may be time to make our wish list.

Going to the tree farm is one of those family traditions that we love because it brings us back to basics. Every year it gives our families at least two new pages in the photo album—helping us track our lives and our children's growing years, gluing us together.

We only need our hatchet, good thick gloves, and sturdy boots, then we can move easily over snowy paths as we search for the perfect Christmas tree. It is the same scene for families all over New England—from Grafton, Vermont, to Sturbridge, Massachusetts.

Our bright woolens punctuate the snowy green-and-white scene. We watch and smile as our children's giggles make puffy cloud trails in the air when they run to that rounded, waiting tree.

This beloved ritual is a holiday of its very own. And tree farmers all over the six-state region ready themselves for the happy invasion, anticipating the snow paths that will come, fresh and piney, as the chosen trees come down and are taken across the snow. It's

The ritual of choosing and cutting down your own Christmas tree is cherished by New Englanders of all ages.

The nursery for Christmas trees is an easy one to spot. Short, squat trees all in a line, row after row, acre after acre. Someday, when they're tall enough, they'll wait for a small chubby hand to grab and bow and holler, "This one. I want this one, Mom."

been over one hundred and fifty years since Mark Carr hauled two ox sleds full of trees from the Catskills to the streets of New York and opened the very first retail tree lot in the United States.

We take the chosen tree home, shake it down, and move it to our living room—to the bay window or the corner near the fireplace. It gets center stage. Dusty boxes marked "Christmas decorations" are soon carried down from the attic. We string the lights and the popcorn, hook and hang decorations, and roll the blanket around the base, readying it for the gifts to come.

In the picturesque little town of Sutton, Massachusetts, thirty artists who hand-paint Christmas decorations all year get ready for the new season. This is Vaillancourt Folk Art, one of a handful of America's remaining Christmas ornament and collectible makers. They paint more than three hundred versions of Santa and Father Christmas figures, all made from antique nineteenth-century chocolate molds—a process that is the brainchild of artist Judi Vaillancourt. Every February, when she brings out her new Santas, there are collec-

tors camped in the driveway, waiting for the first ten of the numbered collectibles.

Craftspeople all over New England work year-round preparing for the holiday season, and those not making decorations are making things that just might end up under the Christmas tree.

On Swan's Island, Maine, John and Carolyn Grace spend every day making Swan's Island all-wool blankets from their own looms, often with wool from their flocks of sheep. Handmade wares find their way to the Women's Educational and Industrial Union in Boston this season.

In the quaint town of Dorset, Vermont, at Flower Brook Pottery, designer Janno Gay spends many a day painting pottery or creating new patterns for a new season. And at Creative Hands Inc. in Salisbury, Connecticut, artists bring their hand-knit items and handmade pottery and jewelry for the holidays.

New England's unique character gives craftspeople plenty of inspiration, and the artists give New England much to touch, see, and cherish—and pass on to loved ones by way of the Christmas tree.

THE BEST PLACE TO BE

Snowbound

Winter in New England can last from November through April, six months of snowy weather, sleet storms, and rawness. If you live in a city, like Boston, Massachusetts, by the ocean, chances are you will see less snow than an inland city like Worcester. And for city dwellers, winter can just mean a change of scenery. People are still around. Urbanites may get a little tired of the cold and wind, but their experience pales to what residents of Craftsbury, Vermont, will endure. Winter in the countryside transforms the view and the people. Life changes with the anticipation of snowfall.

When people do errands, they stock up the freezer and cupboards because there will undoubtedly, some point soon, be a good foot or two of snow making them housebound. If they depend on a wood-burning stove for heat, the wood comes in, or at least closer to the house for easy reach. The candle supply gets checked, since losing electricity in an ice storm is as predictable as the sun coming up. With that, the beds get layered with extra blankets, and drafty areas get sealed.

To get through the cold and the isolation that comes with weather that holds us indoors, cities and towns work hard to bring the people together with church suppers, theater shows, concerts, snow-shoeing parties, and sleigh rides.

It's a good time, too, for the craftspeople to hole up and make products in their workshops at home. From potters to furniture makers, this is the time to take a breath, focus a fresh eye, and invent a new look, a new piece, a new color theme.

For some, it's a time to try something new to get us through the winter blahs. First-time knitters will find locally spun wool and classes to help them create their inaugural project. Resorts and inns may offer cooking or winemaking classes to get people out and mingling. Experts on antiques or cake decorating may come in for a special lecture. Local artists may open their studios and offer classes in painting or photography.

Winter is also a time when New Englanders entertain at home. Having a warm fire going and a homemade

The snowy roads make it tough to get too far in the winter. This cozy farm-house makes the snowbound days pleasant and warm.

meal for friends fills many a dreary-weather weekend. Hearty soups, stews, and crusty breads come to the table. Dessert pies arrive warm with homemade ice cream melting down the sides. We bring out the cappuccino maker, spice sticks for hot apple cider, and our cookie jars, which fill up with homemade goodies.

To make our homes warm and inviting, we often alter our decor and palettes to accommodate the season. This old homestead's palette keeps the cold out with warm paint hues and rich-colored rugs and accents. Many New Englanders follow this design ritual. What was once a cool, bare wood floor may get topped by a few colorful rugs to add warmth. Electric light gets supplemented with candlelight. Summery curtains get swapped for darker, heavier ones that frame a snowy scene. The light cotton bedcover is exchanged for something of substance. A fireplace mantel or windowsill that was once lined with seashells now bears a colorful collection of carved wood birds or a rainbow of hand-blown glass. We may change our art too, just to give us new inside views.

There are lots of ways we can bring color and new spirit into our spaces. It can be as simple as lining a paper-white shelf with antique books that have burnt red or bright blue spines, swapping a solid lampshade to a floral one, or accenting a room with a new wallpaper border.

For ideas, take a trip to Kent, Connecticut, and visit Shandell's at 27 Railroad Street (or www.shandell.com), which sells hand-crafted lampshades, pillows, mirrors, and home accents with vintage wallpaper and fabrics from 1890 to 1945. Or try Barbara Fine Associates in Beverly, Massachusetts (www.bfineart.com), for a stunning collection of antique prints and maps. There are colorful botanicals, fruits, nautical scenes, fashion items, and maps from the 1600s to the 1900s, perfectly preserved. Fill a wall with Fine's nature and floral prints and erase the gloom of the fifth day of snow.

To see one of the finest examples of New England charm visit the nineteenth-century Cannondale Village in Wilton, Connecticut. Here, on a tiny plot of land no bigger than a half a city block, are a handful of shops, a gallery that will inspire, and goods that will easily find their way into the car. Annabel Green specializes in fresh and dried flowers, topiaries, wreaths, and unusual home goods. Greenwillow Antiques offers one-of-a-kind designed items, from furniture to fabrics. The Cannondale Gallery promotes the work of local artists.

THE COZY

Ski House

Anyone who does not ski prays the snowfall will be swift and short. Everyone else, however, creates little altars of hope at the mudroom door with skis and poles gathered into a corner, where they can be grabbed for a quick escape to the slopes.

Visions of ten inches of powder dance in skiers' heads. They dream of that first morning's snow, light and fluffy, when they ski out the back door of the lodge and put down the first tracks. And they live for that end-of-the-day glow on their cheeks, that winter tan, and that great feeling of being spent. They come from the slopes, an army of snow fiends fanned out against the snow-drifts and trails, surreal peacock tails moving in unison. Soon their bodies will sink into a couch by the fire.

When they can, New Englanders search for the per-fect plot of land for a ski getaway, or an old house that needs some tender loving care to bring it back to life. The key, of course, is to be near the slopes, if not just off one. You can find these domestic treasures on the sides of mountains, off steep, winding roads, or deep in the woods. Nearly every state in the region boasts great places to downhill ski, and you can be sure to see snow traffic start the minute the snow forecast ends.

Many New England architects are masters at creating the perfect ski lodge atmosphere with rustic materials and an eye toward making these homes into warm, inviting places to be for long, snowy weekends in the country. The components might include stone- or brick-floored entry areas that will store ski and snow gear; wood cubbies with pegs to hold the snow-encrusted parkas, mittens, and scarves, and radiant-heated floors to warm us. An outdoor, wood-stoked sauna is not unheard of out here, and, for the brave, neither is the outdoor shower—for that back-to-nature thrill and instant wake-me-up.

We love our snow escapes and dream all year long of that morning we'll wake up, buried in white powder.

And let's not forget the fireplaces—the center-piece of the main room—often built from local stone. Sometimes they reach across and up a wall, adding a glow to the great room, an open dining area that allows everyone to stay together to share ski stories and hot ciders all around.

Ski cabins are casual, comfortable places where old wool throws sit on each couch or loveseat, where the wood is piled high on either end of the fireplace, and where the walls might be adorned with a collage of ten years' worth of photos recording great ski parties. Another wall might display a handful of wooden sleds—adding color while being practical.

An old family hand-me-down leather sofa and matching chair, and wool-covered couch might constitute the furnishings, keeping the place cozy. To make the mood sweet, or sometimes romantic, a collection of old sconces and candles could line the halls, and a real candelabra might hang over an antique farm table where ten skiers can congregate for meals. Reclaimed church benches might be the preferred seating around the table. Colorful wool blankets may be transformed into curtains by simply clipping them to rings on rods.

Kitchen countertops might all be butcher block so when a party of six is all together preparing food, every-one can chop together. The kitchen floor could be brick, and there might even be a drain in the center for easy cleaning after a party.

The log home, post-and-beam structure, barn-turned-lodge, and stone house all become part of the ski lodge inventory here—all with plenty of windows wrapping the space to take in the scenery. Depending on the budgets, local craftspeople might be called in to make a custom staircase and railing that has a ski theme carved into it, or to hand-paint some tile that suggests the same.

Those looking for smaller places with equally rich character may seek the counsel of architects such as Maine's Bob Knight, who is known for Lucia's Little Houses (www.luciaslittlehouses.com). Some of these tiny getaways are only 650 square feet, but each of them, in true New England fashion, display the qualities of the region in its architecture and design details.

To capture the feeling of another era, we might hunt down themed items to decorate our walls—every-thing from antique postcards from New England's old resorts to old skis and poles that will give a guest bed-room a design kick and a little texture. The hunt can begin at a place like the United House Wrecking Company in Connecticut.

The fireplace is the anchor of the ski lodge. It's where we gather to share stories of the day and warm up after a day spent in the cold.

There are many ways to experience winter's magical spell, and each gives us one-of-a-kind moments with snow. Strap on your cross-country skis and take off midday, when the sun is at its warmest on your face. The blue-sky canvas anchored in white, the whiz of wood cutting through snow, and your lungs taking in the frigid air: It is the perfect vignette. Step into a horse-drawn sleigh in Vermont, wrap yourself in a woolly blanket, and take in the magnificence of a rolling pasture iced in thick mounds of snow. If it's sunset and the sky is washed in pink and red, the snow will look like silk blowing across the hills. Winter in New England is poetry for the eyes.

Take a winter weekend at a New England inn and experience the season's snow like you never have before. Head for the Balsams in New Hampshire or the 1811 House or Twin Farms in Vermont. Rise early for a breakfast of pancakes and muffins before trekking off with your snowshoes or cross-country skis. And once you feel spent, head back to the inn for a hot chocolate by the fire.

Stop by the local grocery store one winter morning and pick up supplies for a day on the snowmobile trails. You can count on these establishments to have everything you need to get you through the day—from an extra set of mittens to a hearty submarine sandwich for lunch. And if you stick around for a fresh pot of coffee to finish brewing, you'll hear the weather news mixed in with a bit of political banter. These places are often home to the best news team around.

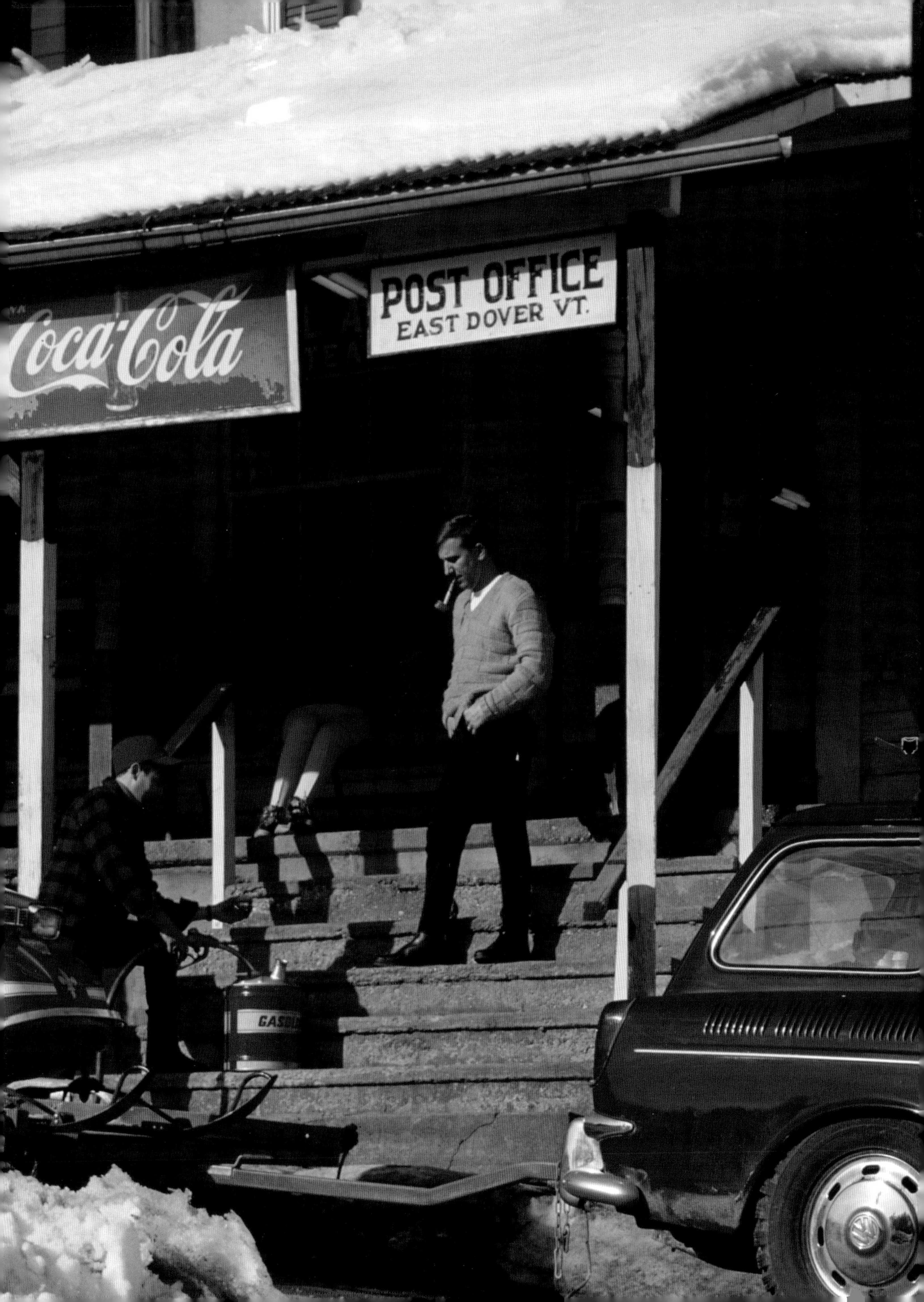

Coca-Cola
POST OFFICE
EAST DOVER VT.

Connecticut

Inns

Bee & Thistle Inn
100 Lyme Street
Old Lyme, CT 06371
860-434-1667
www.beeandthistleinn.com

The Boulders Inn
Lakeshore Road
New Preston, CT 06777
860-868-0541

Cotswold Inn
76 Myrtle Avenue
Westport, CT 06880
203-226-3766

Chimney Crest Manor
Five Founders Drive
Bristol, CT 06010
860-582-4219

Cornwall Inn
US 7
Cornwall Bridge, CT
06754
800-786-6884

Curtis House
(Connecticut's oldest inn)
CT 6
Woodbury, CT 06798
203-263-2101

Griswold Inn
36 Main Street
Essex, CT 06426
860-767-1776
www.griswoldinn.com

Inn at Mystic
Rt. 1 & 27
Mystic, CT 06355
860-536-9604
www.innatmystic.com

The Inn at National Hall
Two Post Road
Westport, CT 06880
203-221-1351

Lighthouse Inn
Six Guthrie Place
New London, CT
888-443-8411 (toll free)
www.lighthouseinn-ct.com

The Mayflower Inn
118 Woodbury Road
CT 47, Washington
860-868-9466

Old Riverton Inn
CT 20, north of Winsted
Riverton, CT 06065
860-379-8678

Stonehenge Inn
35 Stonehenge Road
US 7
Ridgefield, CT 06877
203-438-6511
www.stonehengeinn.com

Wake Robin Inn
Rte 41 Sharon Road
Lakeville, CT 06039
860-435-2000

Water's Edge
1525 Boston Post Road
Westbrook, CT 06498
860-399-5901
www.watersedge-
resort.com

West Lane Inn
22 West Lane
Ridgefield, CT 06877
203-438-7323
www.westlaneinn.com

White Hart
CT 41 & 44
Salisbury, CT
860-435-0030

Attractions

Barnum Museum
820 Main St.
Bridgeport, CT 06610
203-331-1104
www.barnummuseum.org

Beardsley Zoological
Gardens
1875 Noble Ave.
Bridgeport, CT 06610
203-394-6565
www.beardsleyzoo.org

Bellamy-Ferriday House
& Gardens
Nine Main Street
Bethlehem
203-266-7596

Bob Ellis Coach &
Carriage Service
(carriage, sleigh
& stagecoach rides)
62 Deer Lane
Morris, CT
860-567-1114

Caprilands Herb Farm
534 Silver Street
Coventry, CT
860-742-7244

The Corn Maze
at White Hollow Farm
RTE 7 & 112
Lime Rock, CT
860-824-0497

Cornwall Bridge
Pottery Store
CT 128
West Cornwall, CT
860-672-6545

Hillstead Museum
35 Mountain Rd.
Farmington, CT 06032
860-677-9064
www.hillstead.org

Hitchcock Chair Company
and Factory Store
CT 20
Riverton, CT

Hotchkiss-Flyer House
192 Main Street
Torrington, CT
860-482-8260

Lee's Riding Stable Inc.
57 East Litchfield Rd.
Litchfield, CT
860-567-0785

Lockwood-Matthews
Mansion
295 West Ave.
Norwalk, CT
203-838-1434

Lyman Orchards
(one of America's oldest
working farms)
CT 147 & 157,
Middlefield, CT
860-349-1793

Maple View Farm
603 Oranges Center Road
Orange, CT

Mark Twain Memorial
at Nook Farm
351 Farmington Avenue
Hartford, CT
860-493-6411

New England
Carousel Museum
Riverside Ave.
Bristol, CT
860-585-5411

Ogden House & Gardens
1520 Bronson Rd
Fairfield, CT 06430
203-259-1598

Roseland Cottage
CT 169
Woodstock, CT
860-928-4074

Wadsworth Atheneum
600 Main Street
Hartford, CT
860-278-2670

Maine

Inns

Black Point Inn
510 Black Point Road
Prouts Neck, ME 04074
207-883-4126
www.blackpointinn.com

The Birches Resort
Rockwood, ME
800-825-9453

Boothbay Island, ME
(68-acre island and mansion
to rent)
www.jgreer@unusualvil-
larentals.com

Cape Arundel Inn
Ocean Ave.
Kennebunkport, ME
207- 967-2125

Captain Lord Mansion
(Corner of Green & Pleasant St.)
Kennebunkport, ME
04046
207-967-3141
www.captainlord.com

Cliff House
Shore Road
Ogunquit, ME 03907
207-361-1000
www.cliffhousemaine.com

The Colony Hotel
Ocean Ave.
Kennebunkport, ME
800-55-2363

Dark Harbor House
Islesboro, ME
207-734-6669
www.darkharborhouse.com

Fox Island Inn
Carver Street
Vinalhaven Island, ME
207-863-2122

The Green Heron
126 Ocean Ave.
Kennebunkport, ME
207-967-3315
www.info@green-
heroninn.com

Inn at Tanglewood Hall
611 York Street
York Harbor, ME 03911
207-363-7577

Island Inn
Monhegan Island, ME
04852
207-596-0371

The Keeper's House
Isle au Haut, ME
207-367-2261

Norumbega
61 High Street
Camden, ME
207-236-4646

Pomegranate Inn
49 Neal Street
Portland, ME 04102
207-772-1006

White Barn Inn
37 Beach Avenue
Kennebunkport, ME
04046
207-967-2321

Attractions

American Eagle
Windjammer Cruise
Rockland, ME
800-648-4544

Maine Maritime Museum
243 Washington St.
Bath, ME 04563
207-443-1316
www.bathmaine.com

Maine Photographic
Workshops
Rockport, ME
207-236-8581

Maine Sport Outfitters
Rockport, ME
207-236-8797

The Migis Lodge
South Casco, ME
207-653-4524

Moosehead Marine
Museum
Greenville, ME
207-695-2716

Nichols-Sortwell House
Corner of Main
& Federal Streets
Wiscasset, ME

The Olsen House
(Where Andrew Wyath painted)
Hathron Point Road
Cushing, ME
207-596-6457

Prout's Neck Cliff Path
& Wildlife Sanctuary
Rte.9
207-646-0226
(near Winslow Homer's studio)

The Schooner
Stephen Tabor
Windjammer Wharf
Rockland, ME 04841
207-236-3520
www.stephentabor.com

Massachusetts

Inns

Boston Harbor Hotel
Rowes Wharf
Boston, MA
617-439-7000
www.bhh.com

The Charles Hotel
One Bennett St.
Cambridge, MA
617-864-1200

Charlotte Inn
27 South Summer St.
Martha's Vineyard, MA
02539
508-627-4751

The Colonial Inn
48 Monument Sq.
Concord, MA
508-369-9200

Deerfield Inn
81 Old Main St.
Deerfield, MA 01342
413-774-5587
www.deerfieldinn.com

The Eliot Hotel
370 Commonwealth
Avenue
Boston, MA
617-267-1607

Field Farm Guest House
554 Sloan Road
Willaimstown, MA
413-458-3135

The Harbor Light Inn
58 Washington Street
Marblehead, MA
781-631-2186

Hawthorne Hotel
18 Washington Square
West
Salem, MA
978-7444080

Hotel Meridian
250 Franklin
Boston, MA
617-451-1900

Inn at Castle Hil
280 Argilla Rd.
Ipswich, MA 01938
987-921-1944
www.innatcastlehill.com

Longfellow's Wayside Inn
Wayside Inn Road
Sudbury, MA
508-443-1776
www.wayside.org

Miles River Country Inn
823 Bay Road
Hamilton, MA
97

The Old Inn on the Green
Rte. 57
New Marlborough, MA
800-286-3139
www.oldinn.com

Red Lion Inn
30 Main St.
Stockbridge, MA 01250
www.redlioninn.com

Salt Marsh Farm
322 Smith Neck Rd.
So. Dartmouth, MA
02748
508-992-0980

The Summer House
Siasconset
Nantucket
508-257-4577

Wheatleigh
Hawthorne Rd.
Lenox, MA
413-637-0610

Attractions

The Agawam Diner
Rte. 1 & 133, Rowley

Bearskin Neck
Rockport, MA

Beauport
Eastern Point
E. Gloucester, MA
978-283-0800

The Boston Public Garden
Arlington Street
Boston, MA

Cranberry World
Visitor's Center
Water Street
Plymouth, MA
508-746-2350

The Crane Estate
Argilla Road
Ipswich, MA
(magnificent mansion & beach)

Essex Shipbuilding
Museum
28 Main Street
Essex, MA
978-768-7541

Fruitlands Museums
102 Prospect Hill Road
Harvard, MA
(the Alcott family's experiment
in communal living)

Goodale Orchards
Argilla Road
Ipswich, MA

Hancock Shaker Village
US 20
413-443-0188

Historic Deerfield
Old Deerfield, MA
www.historic-deerfield.org

The Ipswich Clambox
Rte. 1-A North
Ipswich, MA

Marine Museum
70 Water Street
Battleship Cove
Fall River, MA
508-674-3533

Mayflower II
State Pier
Plymouth, MA

Motif #1
The red shed off Bearskin
Neck
Rockport, MA
(painted and photographed by
thousands!)

Naumkeag
Prospect Hill Road
Stockbridge, MA
413-298-3239

The New Bedford Whaling
Museum
18 Johnny Cake Square
New Bedford, MA 02740
508-997-0046
www.whalingmuseum.org

Norman Rockwell
Museum
9 Glendale Road
Stockbridge, MA 02162
800-742-9450

Old Sturbridge Village
One Old Sturbridge
Village Rd.
Sturbridge, MA 01566
508-347-3362
www.osv.org

Paper House
Pigeon Hill Street
Rockport, MA
(house made of newspaper)

The Peabody Essex
Museum
East India Square
Salem, MA 01970
978-745-9500

Pilgrim Hall Museum
74 Court St.
Plymouth, MA
508-746-1620

Plimouth Plantation
3-A
Plymouth, MA
978-746-1622

Plymouth Rock
Water Street
Plymouth, MA

Public clambakes at
Francis Farms
Rehoboth, MA
508-252-3212

Rotch-Jones-Duff House
& Garden Museum
365 County Street
New Bedford, MA
508-997-1401

Salem Witch Museum
19 1/2 Washington St.
Salem, MA
508-744-1692

The Shaker Shop
454 Main St., US 20
Sturbridge, MA

Tanglewood Music
Festival
Lenox, MA
413-637-1600

Wenham Teahouse
4 Monument St.
Wenham, MA
978-468-1235
www.wenhamteahouse.com

New Hampshire

Inns

Ames Farm Inn
2800 Lake Shore Road
Gilford, NH 03246
603-293-4321
www.amesfarminn.com

The Balsams
Rte. 26
Dixville Notch, NH 03576
800-255-0600
www.thebalsams.com

Castle Springs
Moultonborough, NH
03254
603-476-2352
www.castlesprings.com

The Inn
at Strawberry Bank
314 Concord St.
Portsmouth, NH 03801
603-436-7242

The John Hancock Inn
33 Main St.
Hancock, NH 03449
www.hancockinn.com

The Manor
on Golden Pond
Squam Lake, Rt. 3
Holderness, NH 03245
www.manorongolden-
pond.com

Philbrook Farm Inn
881 North Road
Shelburne, NH 03501
603-466-3831

Rockhouse Mountain
Farm Inn
Eaton Center, NH
603-447-2880

The Wentworth Resort
Hotel
Jackson, NH 03846
603-383-9700
www.thewentworth.com

Attractions

Fuller Gardens
10 Willow Ave.
Little Boar's Head, N.
Hampton
603-964-5414

New England Ski Museum
P.O.Box 267
Franconia Notch, NH
800-639-4181
www.skimuseum.org

The Robert Frost Place
Ridge Road, off Rte 116
Franconia, NH
603-823-8038g

Rundlett-May House
Middle Street
Portsmouth, NH 03801
603-436-3205

The Saint- Gaudens
National Historic Site
Rte. 12-A
Cornish, NH
603-675-2175

Strawberry Banke
Museum
Portsmouth, NH
603-433-1100
(a preserved neighborhood)

Wentworth-Coolidge
Mansion
Little Harbor Road
Portsmouth, NH 03801
603-436-6607

Wentworth-Gardener &
Tobias Lear Houses
Gardener and Mechanic
Streets
Portsmouth, NH 03801
603-436-4406

Rhode Island

Inns

Admiral Fitzroy Inn
398 Thames St.
Newport, RI 02840
401-848-8000
www.admiralfitzroy.com

The Atlantic Inn
High St. (Old Harbor)
Block Island, RI 02807
401-466-5883
800-224-7422

Cliffside Inn
2 Seaview Ave.
Newport, RI 02840
401-847-1811
www.cliffsideinn.com

The Francis Malbone
House
392 Thames St.
Newport, RI 02890
401-846-0392
www.malbone.com

Joseph Reynolds House
956 Hope St.
Bristol, RI 02809
401-254-0230
(circa 1693)

The Roost
Sakonnet Vineyards
162 West Main Road
Little Compton, RI 02837
401-635-8486

Vanderbuilt Hall
41 Mary Street
Newport, RI 02840

Attractions

Blithwold Mansion
& Gardens
101 Ferry Rd.
Bristol, RI 02809
401-253-2707
www.blithwold.org

The Breakers
Bellevue Ave.
Newport, RI 02840
401-847-1000

Green Animals
380 Corey's Lane
Newport, RI 02840
401-683-1267

Herreshoff Marine
Museum
One Burnside St.
Bristol, RI 02808
401-253-5000

International Tennis Hall
of Fame
194 Bellevue Ave.
Newport, RI 02840
800-457-1144
www.tennisfame.com

Linden Place Museum
500 Hope St.
Bristol, RI 02809
401-253-0390
www.lindenplace.org

Museum of Yachting
Fort Adams
Newport, RI 02840
401-847-1018
www.moy.org

Sakonnet Vineyards*
162 West Main St.
Little Compton, RI 02837
800-91WINES
www.sakonnetwine.com
* Go to page??? for other NE
vineyards

Vermont

Inns

Basin Harbor Club
Lake Champlain
Vergennes, VT 05491
800-622-4000
www.basinharbor.com

Bates Mansion
at Brook Farm
20 Mile Stream Rd.
Cavendish, VT 05142
802-226-7863
www.batesmansion.com

The Dorset Inn
8 Church Street
Dorset, Vermont 05251
877-367-7384

1811 House
Manchester Village
Manchester, VT 05254
www.1811house.com

The Equinox
Rte. 7-A
Manchester Village, VT
05253
802-362-1595
www.equinoxresort.com

Four Columns Inn
On the Green
Newfane, VT 05345
800-787-6633
www.fourcolumnsinn.com

Heermansmith Farm Inn
Heermanville Road
Coventry, VT 05825
802-754-8866

The Inn at Mountain
View Creamery
Darling Hill Road
East Burke, VT 05832
802-626-9924

The Inn at Sawmill Farm
P.O.Box 367
West Dover, VT 05356
802-464-8131
www.theinnatsawmill-
farm.com

Inn at Shelburne Farms
1611 Harbor Rd.
Shelburne, VT 05482
802-985-8498
www.shelburnefarms.org

The Inn on the Common
Craftsbury Common
Craftsbury, VT 05827
800-521-2233

Naulakha
Brattleboro, VT
802-254-6868
(historic landmark once home
of Rudyard Kipling)

The Old Tavern at Grafton
92 Main St.
Grafton, VT 05146
www.windham-founda-
tion.org

Reluctant Panther
17-34 West Rd.
Manchester, VT 05254
www.reluctantpanther.com

Trapp Family Lodge
700 Trapp Hill Rd.
Stowe, VT 05672
800-253-8511
www.trappfamily.com

Twin Farms
P.O.Box 115
Barnard, VT 05031
802-234-9999
www.twinfarms.com

Woodstock Inn
Fourteen The Green
Woodstock, VT 05091
800-448-7900
www.woodstockinn.com

Attractions

American Museum
of Fly Fishing
3657 Main St.
Manchester, VT 05254
802-362-3300
www.amff.com

Billings Farm & Museum
Rt. 12
Woodstock, VT 05091
802-457-2355
www.billingsfarm.org

Blue Slate Farm
Crown Point Road
Bridgeport, Vermont
802-758-2577

Champlain Chocolates
750 Pine Street
Burlington, VT 05401
800-465-5909
www.lakechamplainchoco-
lates.com

Eastman Long & Sons
Sugarhouse
1188 Tucker Hill Road
Waitsfield, VT
802-496-3448

Hildene
Rt. 7A
Manchester, VT 05254
802-362-1788
www.hildene.org

Lake Champlain Maritime
Museum
4472 Basin Harbor Rd.
Vergennes, VT 05491
802-475-2022
www.lcmm.org

Maple Ridge Sheep Farm
P.O. Box 147
Randolph, VT 05060
802-728-3081
www.mrsf.com

Naulakha
481 Kipling Rd.
Dummerston, VT 05346
802-254-6868

New England Maple
Museum
P.O.Box 1615
Rutland, VT 05701
802-483-9414
www.maplemuseum.com

Norman Rockwell
Museum
Rte 4
Rutland, VT
802-773-6095
Sugar House Directory
www.vermontmaple.org

The Organic Cow of
Vermont
Tunbridge, VT
802-685-3123

The Park-McCullough
House
Rte. 67-A
N. Bennington, VT
802-442-5441

Redrock Farm
53-A Strafford Turnpike
Chelsea, VT
(pick your own Christmas tree
for UPS delivery)

Robert Frost House
121 Historic Rt. 7A
Shaftsbury, VT 05262
802-447-6200
www.frostfriends.org

Shelburne Farms
1611 Harbor Rd.
Shelburne, VT 05482
802-985-8686
www.shelburnefarms.org

The UVM Morgan
Horse Farm
Rte. 23
Weybridge Street
Middlebury, VT
802-388-2011

The Vermont Craft Center
at Frog Hollow
Middlebury, VT
802-388-3177

Vermont Icelandic
Horse Farm
RR-376-1
Waitsfield
802-496-7141

Wilson Castle
P.O.Box 190
Rutland, VT 05736
802-773-3284
www.wilsoncastle.com

Reference Sources

Brown, Ben, "Nantucket Tradition", *Coastal Living*, September 2002, 100–107

Colman, David, "Atlantic High", *Elle Décor*, November 2002, 187–192

Kasabian, Anna, "Centennial Cottage", *Coastal Living*, July–August, 2002, 82–86

Mera, Phyllis Mera & Tom Gannon. *Rhode Island, An Explorer's Guide*, © 1995 Countryman Press

Nangle, Hilary, M., "Not Your Ordinary Cabin by the Lake", *New England Travel & Life*, Fall–Winter 2001–2002, 31–37

New England Insight Guide, © 1984

Older, Jules, "A Little Bit Country", *New England Travel & Life*, Spring–Summer 2001, 60–65

Porter, Paige, Main Stay, July–August 2001, *Coastal Living*, 113–116

Tree, Christina, & Barbara J. Beeching. *Connecticut, An Explorer's Guide*, © 1994, CountrymanPress

Tree, Christina, & Elizabeth Roundy. *Maine, An Explorer's Guide* © 1982 Countryman Press

Tree, Christina & William Davis. *Massachusetts, An Explorer's Guide*, © 1996 Countryman Press

Tree, Christina & Peter Randall. *New Hampshire, An Explorer's Guide*, © 1991 Countryman Press

Tree, Christina & Peter Jennison. *Vermont, An Explorer's Guide*, © 1983 Countryman Press

August 12, 1999 Wiscasset Newspaper, "Expert Clammer Offers Tips for Seaside Gleaners" Vol. 30–No. 32 (Internet article:www.wiscassetnewspaper.maine.com)

Internet sites

www.vaics.org/vaics–dorset
http://peltiersmarket.com
www.thecountrystorevt.com
www.taftsville.com

Illustration Credits

Walter Bibikow 32, 80, 94

Malcolm Brooks 84

Patricia J. Bruno 155

Kindra Cliniff 5, 12, 22, 23, 27, 29, 30, 37, 51, 52, 53, 56, 58, 69, 76, 82, 83, 85, 86, 88, 89, 90, 98, 100, 101, 107, 108, 111, 114, 124, 125, 130, 132, 134, 138, 148, 150, 159, 160, 161, 163, 164, 170, 172, 187, 188, 191, 192, 194, 196, 197, 207, 208, 209, 213, 215

Corbis 17, 61, 66, 67, 110, 111, 117, 127, 142, 179

John Elk III 153, 156, 162, 174

Sara Gray 145, 147

Jeff Greenberg 32

John Gruen 74, 75

John M. Hall, courtesy of Twin Farms 210, 211

Robert Holmes 28, 32, 33, 68, 96, 122, 135, 154, 171, 186

Anna Kasabian 24, 138, 140, 141

David Kasabian 38, 78, 110, 111, 139

Jack McConnell 20, 92, 111, 112, 154, 155

Retrofile.com 212

Paul Rocheleau 4, 6, 11, 19, 23, 47, 125, 128, 131, 132, 133, 167, 168, 169, 172, 173, 188, 189, 202,

Eric Roth 48, 54, 103, 104, 105, 106, 118, 120, 121, 137, 173, 181, 182, 183, 184, 185, 189, 224

Pam Spaulding 126

Tommy Hilfiger Inc., courtesy of 126

Brian Vanden Brink 3, 8, 14, 34, 36, 37, 41, 42, 43, 44, 45, 59, 62, 64, 120, 146, 176, 198, 200, 201, 204, 206

William Waldron 71, 72, 73

Woodman's, courtesy of 77